SAMUEL CHIBUISI JOB

The Power of Positive Mind

SAMUEL CHIBUISI JOB

The Power of Positive Mind

Unveiling Productivity vs Value

JustFiction Edition

Imprint

Any brand names and product names mentioned in this book are subject to trademark, brand or patent protection and are trademarks or registered trademarks of their respective holders. The use of brand names, product names, common names, trade names, product descriptions etc. even without a particular marking in this work is in no way to be construed to mean that such names may be regarded as unrestricted in respect of trademark and brand protection legislation and could thus be used by anyone.

Cover image: www.ingimage.com

Publisher:
JustFiction! Edition
is a trademark of
Dodo Books Indian Ocean Ltd., member of the OmniScriptum S.R.L Publishing group
str. A.Russo 15, of. 61, Chisinau-2068, Republic of Moldova Europe
Printed at: see last page
ISBN: 978-620-3-57535-4

THE POWER OF POSITIVE MIND
{Unveiling Productivity vs Value }

SAMUEL C. JOB

AMAZON E-KINDLE BOOK PUBLICATIONS
&
MOREBOOKS.DE PUBLICATION

" One major tragedy of Today's Generation is discovered in the misuse, mismanagement, abuse and misunderstanding of the greatest assets given to humanity by divinity called the MIND." Samuel c. Job.

Table Of Contents

Dedication — 3

Forward — 3

Introduction — 8

Chapter one
Status of The mind — 13

Chapter Two
Positive Thinking, Negative Thinking and Right Thinking — 21

Chapter Three
Few Nuggets On The Mind In Creating Values — 36

Chapter Four
Create A value More Than Your Volume — 48

Chapter Five
Change is Powerful — 56

Chapter Six
Review Your Routine — 68

Chapter Seven
Stir Up The Gift In And Within YOU — 87

Chapter Eight
Few nuggets to review about your mind — 109

Chapter Nine
Words Of Wisdom — 129

About The Book — 133

About The Author — 134

DEDICATION

This book is dedicated to the Holy Spirit, my guide, my senior mentor, comforter, inspirer and Ebenezer. To my wonderful, sweet parents (Mr & Mrs Owhondah I.), my siblings: Obodo, Onyeoma, Obiageri ,Emmanuel .

The dedication cannot be complete if I fail to mention a friend, Obianuju Emereum Obioma (MPJ) who came into my life 2019 as we reunited after several years not seen and heard from each other , she inspired and reignited the fire in me during the phase one lockdown of the covid –19 with her words ' Sam You have so much content' and this word have produced and taken me to connect deeper with lives and impact more and it also gave rise to my official fan page with over 5000 followers on Facebook today.

And my thanks can not be complete without mentioning my admirable ever standing friend and brother and team Admin, Mr. Simeon Uboh O.

My bigger thanks also goes to all my senior coaches, mentors , teachers , associates and counselors and professors who in one way or the other reviewed , recommended, contributed   in forwarding this piece , am forever humbled and grateful . Thanks Sir/ Ma.

You are my Aaron sir .   Thank you for your unwavering love and support. You are my best treasure.

Also to you, the reader, my personal prayer is that as you go through this piece, God will cause you to obtain Rhema to have a mental drastic shift and cause your life and relationship to take a greater impact in Jesus name. Amen!

FORWARDS < Reviews and Recommendation >

"It is all in your head!" this is what the author is trying to subliminally convey as a message to his readers.

Mindset is of the utmost importance when it comes to reality perception and the possibilities of self-improvement we allow ourselves to have. And it lies within our power to change any shortcomings or painful situations for that matter.

There is a solution to any problem and the key to overcome any hardships and go beyond the average life is change. Clinging on to our comfort zone does nothing but keep us prisoners inside the same vicious circle of routine and plateau stage. But why is change so difficult to achieve? Because many times answers are just in front of our own eyes and, any human being may guess, irrespective of his/ her IQ, that a positive mind-frame is always better than a negative one, and that "adjusting your vision is inevitable in pursuing your dreams", as the author, Job Samuel, so beautifully puts it.

This small yet powerful book offers some invaluable insights and guidance building up around a philosophical concept of the ancient Greeks: Know thyself! It is actually a modern rewriting of the philosophy of self-knowledge(Greek: Gnothi seauton !, Latin: Nosce te ipsum!) This is one of the best known thoughts, which entered the cultural consciousness of the world through its philosophical and moral significance, transmitting an exhortation related to the spiritual dimension of man.

The origin of the expression *know thyself* is in Greek - *gnothi seauton!* The first to refer in writing to this adage is Plato, in one of his Dialogues - Charmides (or On Wisdom) - a work written around 388 BC. Plato says that this thought is the oldest precept engraved at the entrance to the Temple of Delphi, dedicated to the god Apollo, sanctuary of the famous Oracle, words belonging, according to various historical sources, to the seven sages of Greece - honorary name given to politicians, legislators and philosophers during the before-Socrates Greece.

Plato interpreted the words *know thyself*, from the entrance to the temple at Delphi, as a greeting from the gods to those who came to that place, an exhortation to be wise, temperate, resonating with the other two exhortations at the entrance to temple - 'nothing too much' and 'to guarantee means to ruin yourself'.

But the one who consecrated the expression *know thyself!* is actually Socrates, a philosopher of the Greek antiquity, one of the founders of moral philosophy. Although he left no written work, his thinking was passed down through the centuries by his disciples, with Plato and Xenophon making an essential contribution in this regard.

Hence, the author, Job Samuel, urges his readers to embark upon this thrilling adventure of knowing themselves first, then dare to take steps towards self-improvement in order to real the best version of oneself. A small yet compelling book definitely worth reading!

Senior Lecturer Alina BARBU, Ph.D.

Department of Exact Sciences and Humanities

Constanta Maritime University

Romania, Europe .

At the beginning of the road in his journey as an author, Job Samuel is presents us with a very tonic essay on the Power of the Positive Mind.

With the advent of social media, today's youth is being more and more distracted from their path, by being bombarded with imagery, music and information that encourages an endless and fruitless comparison with one's peers. This is no recipe for a meaningful life, as Job rightfully points out. On the contrary, nihilism is one of the great diseases of today's world and overcoming it is not only a personal struggle but it's also a choice. Samuel encourages readers to go out on a journey of self discovery and self acceptance.

Philosophers from the beginning of recorded life on earth, starting with the Story of Gilgamesh from ancient Babylon and until modern times have been struggling to decipher the meaning of life and of our existence in this world. It is refreshing to read about how a youth of today experiences life and how he optimistically approaches tackling its challenges.

As recognised by Friedrich Nietzsche in his works, society is being evermore impacted by the ever accelerating shift of moral values. This leaves most people disorientated, discouraged and depressed. In today's world Nietzsche rings even more truth.

From a literary point of view, the author has an pleasant writing style using clever analogies, storytelling and personal experience to bring his thoughts to life.

PhD Andrei Murineanu

Constanta Maritime University ,

Mechanical Engineering department

This is one of the books that remind us of the reality of life. It quite informative and educative. In the second chapter of the book,It simplifies your thought towards how you view life.

This book not only help you to know how you understand yourself but also how others understand you.It's a book that gives one the power of positive thinking.

The writer uses the analogy of autopilot which is use in flying a plane to describe life which is outstanding in his illustration.

The book is an eye opener to several principles of life.

I recommend the book for everybody who wants to have good success in life. It is a great work of knowledge.

Pst. John Babajide.   Pst. Mrs Bunmi John BBJ.

Trained Project Manager(United Kingdom).   counsellor , staff United Kingdom

This book is an invitation to take time to look inward and examine one's life and circumstances.

It is our negative perception of things, rather than the things themselves, that brings more affliction

and stalls our success. As soon as we change our perception and – indeed – our response to an

external event, we can attain clear judgement and take full control of our potential.

The author offers nuggets of wisdom to motivate and inspire people to become their better version

and take small, but constant steps towards self-improvement. Similarly, he gives practical advice

to unleash the power of the subconscious mind, to listen to one's intuition and to set the right goals

for all aspects of life.

As soon as we start implementing these changes in our daily life, the author argues, we will begin

to truly understand our purpose and place in the world. We are all capable of change if we are

willing to do the inner work. Just begin the work and the rest will follow – seems to be the silver

lining in this brief, but persuading book.

Prof. Cornel Panait

Rector , Constanta Maritime University

Romania , Europe .

The paper is dynamic and also impressive approach regarding the influence of the neuro-linguistic programming to the reality of our existence. The author is manifesting an original way of writing about the NLP, taking in consideration some important rules and laws. It is very well described the way that the effect and the result of any situation must be equal to the cause. The law of cause and effect has been described in the manner that many of the things that we believed granted from the past experience, groups of people and individuals are not true, but they are all the things that we have imagined as being true, out of our need to survive. The author surprises also the relate between rules and beliefs and describes the relate between rules and beliefs. Those beliefs become limitations. Author is explaining the main causes of experiencing sickness, failure and lack, those being determined often by the limitations of our own minds. Our zone of comfort is described in an original manner by the author as being the place where we are locked into, no matter how destructive it may be. If we were ready to receive the truth, our higher self will always reveal it to us.

Also the author is surprising the law of attraction and the way it is operates with mathematical exactitude. The mind attracts whatever is familiar to itself. It is very important for the readers to understand that they are responsible for the situations generated within their life. A frightened mind will attract frightening experiences; a confused mind will attract more confusion within decisions and existence.

Our deepest inner beliefs are also described very careful by the author in the manner that if you accept yourself as being powerless, you will look to something or someone outside of yourself to fulfill your desires. We could use power or life force in order to create anything that we want in our lives. Conflicts and discontents are also described very interesting by the author. There is no growth without discontent. While it is important to live in the present moment and accept this present time; otherwise it is very important to grow up from where you are. Our higher self always knows what is best for us. All we need is to assert that we want something better than we have right now. The rules of life were also designed correctly by the author: if our life doesn't follow the right way, the cause it is probably the acceptance of some false beliefs. We should consider life as being a game, wrote the author, and the advice is for playing with happiness, abundance and health. In NLP theories we usually affirm that each individual plays a game that she or he sets up and that no one game is necessary better than another. The power of the powerless is an important aspect within the relate between interlocutors, surprised easily by the author.

The main idea of the text proposed is that all human beings are manifested an unlimited power to success and it starts in our ability to control our thoughts. Abundance, healthy and success are for healthy minds. In NLP, if our programs are developed like this, will influence other interlocutors' programs and will determine success.

Assoc. Prof. Phd Simona Mina

Constanta Maritime University

Conosco Samuel c. Job Da 2,3 Anni… , Ho letto questo libro Ed. E' molto interessante, e' una buona dose di positivita' e' andrebbe letto un po' da tutti per cambiare un po' la mentalita' un caro saluto Ai Lettori.

ROBERTO BENVENUTO

Head Chef , Italy.

INTRODUCTION

THE MIND AGAINST CHANGE

Making Reference to Africa Continent, and drawing my pointsof interest from the world like United State of America (USA) and Europe.

Every youth in Africa taking reference of Nigeria is battling and facing what I called internal war with man issues of life due to lots of factors and government policies and corruptions in the social – economy system and such tends to live as a mediocre and exhibit average life ,the challenges such faces pushes him or her into deeper thinking and drawing a comparison from his mates in other continentsand as such becomes so defeated physically not knowing that the origin and beginning of the battle was first fought and lost in the fieldof the body system called THE MIND

In my recent research and discovery , I have noticed and realized that anger and hunger alone doesn't determine success , neither does determination, hope and faith alone compel success, and before you go further and get stranded with the above statement and prone to questions, the reason is because success is not a destination nor a goal the way many have pivoted their minds for it to be , but successis considered as a journey or an adventure which every human entityshould aspire for and to journey through .

Many have in their mindset without considering a MindShift that the more they run and chase after their dreams and vision, the more they get closer to it .But I want to shock you, that the more you chase afteryour dream and goals, the more they chase after you

'' in the universal correlation of law, your dream is not supposed to bechased by you but it's supposed to chase you. ''

SUCCESS MINDSET

From my discovery and researches of success in some nations that arecentralized , it becomes a motivation to gear many especially the youths of this generation into fulfilling the pathways to the adventurecalled SUCCESS but in continents like Africa using Nigeria as the giant of Africa with the world in contraction bringing up the issue of success without proper diagnosing the mindsets and mind capacitieswill only end up in a total demotivation and calling an unknown retrogressive in the joining of the rest.

NUISANCE MINDSET.

Many are yet successful today not because they have not developed the capacities for success but there are many especially youths who have not discovered purpose and because of their fixed mindsets, it isin their low esteem and poverty state, their nuisance character and content can be contained reason is because many who wishes to be successful do not wish to have self – content and self – discipline,

'' success without self –content will lead to sustained pains ''

Nuisance mindsets are considered that in such vulnerable state. To empire such an individual with resources will only be a self-instructedattack upon the society.

SHIFT FOR SUCCESS

At some point you journey in this life of as a youth , you have to discover that your weakest assets or values in life are those physicaland visible traits that can be easily seen by people . But your most valuable assets are those traits and characters that are invisible and not easily seen by humanity and such includes … the quality of yourthinking

…... the quality of your reasoning

…..the sate of your mind content

…..the control damage of the information you have

DON'T GIVE UP MINDSET

As a motivational speaker , it is always easy for us to appear before crowds and speak to them saying to all never to give up and especially as a one who was starting the speaking engagements , I could easily say such words to people without considering if there aremany who wishes to give up in different areas and angles of life ,suchas work ,job, relationships ,

companies and associations and religion and church even give up
on their lovers .

So as I begin to grow I starting reversing and coming to a point
whichI wish to suggest and at this moment I think it is an
academic and coaching misconception and arrogant contempt to
demand from multitudes of people under you who you have not
have one –on –onediagnosis with .

To illustrate and speak to such minds never to give –up because
for me I have come to reconsider that giving –up is. A special
skill , you have to know who and how to give up.

The reason is because as you read through the chapters in this
book   , you may need to give up in at least   the following
areas ,,,,,

,,, some needs to give up on a friend

…. some needs to give up on an environment /community
/country oreven continent

...some needs to give up on a relationship and associations ..

…. some needs to give up on ideas and skills

…..some needs to give up on businesses.

Ecclesiastes 3:1-2   **A Time for Everything**

3 There is a time for everything,
  and a season for every activity under the heavens:
2   a time to be born and a time to die,
  a time to plant and a time to uproot,

  Take note ,, if all you know and have is a fixed mind or a mind
on how to keep holding on and never give up, especially on
negative struggles that drains you , then you will hold on to
what its elasticityhas elapse , you will hold on to what is not
backing you up and you hold on to thing no doubt because you
are an adult but it will be a matter and function of time that you
will released that you have kepton things that you are

meant to have given up on and the in return such will cost you to give up the ghost. In holding on on , the context is that not all ideas can give someideas are to be mortified and some are to be given up on .many relationships today.

Chapter 1

STATUS OF THE MIND

In My Recent quest and search for deeper knowledge and walk in the destiny of humanity   and the university of this great universe that brings us a lot of deep questions with most unanswered even that has displaced in many circumstances the world best skills and expertise of both scientists and technicians and has rendered many great and mighty men and women and nations of the globe powerless and confused   and have landed me into discovering again and again as I have kept on speaking and studying and revealing through my teachings and posts and quotes that , the world we live in today has encountered one major illness which I call the sub-exchange and mind reduction as to gearing the power and effect of the mind and this has led many lives into disaster and have killed many lives even before the physical and spiritual deaths ..

One major tragedy of Today's Generation is discovered in the misuse , mismanagement , abuse and misunderstanding of the greatest assets given to humanity by divinity called the MIND .

The mind   of   many today have being heavily destabilized and brought into stand still   and stagnation and rendered vegetative and as   a result many individuals especially Youths of this generation taking account in the pre- era and post – era of the so – called COVID –19   have lost their COMPASS AND FOCUS   in the journey of their life and which have caused the future of the world to be in a pains and as many cries out if they will still bounce back and pick up the pieces of themselves again and pursue their dreams and goals or will they die in the misery that COVI-19 has brought their way.?

But for you are reading this book now , I have a great news for you and I want you to lift up yours eyes to the sky and discovered that there is still a great hope and future for you , and that you can still take back the ownership of your mind and retain the power of your mind . You are not yet a failure nor a looser until you have concluded so and already given up in your mind . The battle of life is never   fought fist and concur in the physical but in the spiritual realm which is to say that every battle of life is. A battle of the mind , and whosoever that can win the battle of the mind first will always stand strong no matter the circumstances and situation now and always come out victorious.

The mind that came with COVID –19

Taking a concise and precise accounts of this season of uncertainty due to the presence of CORONAVIRUS generally called Covid – 19 , I have   come to the re-adjustment and restructuring of my mind , that the death of life , vision , dreams , goals , ambition , purpose and that the killer of many great power packed businesses , companies , firms and organization and under performance of many countries and continents didn't not just take place nor effect only because of the VIRUS but such happened because of the state of the mind (mental capacity was never properly and adequately set into motion and before any physical death occurs , there precedes a mental death).

Until you win the battle of life in the journey of destiny in the mind first , you can never win the battle Of life physically .

During this season , It was also drawn to my attention, that I must keep recapping and readdressing once again as one of my most frequent collaborative uses of words , because the fuel that generates or degenerates the mind is the CHOICE OF WORDS . So at this junction , I want you to understand that , in   every season and phase of life as generations come and pass,. MEN RISE AND MEN FALL .

The question here should not be ,, WHY ? BUT SHOULD BE HOW ? AND WHERE DID IT ALL BEGIN .... SEARCH OUT AND THINK AGAIN AS SCRIPTURE CAN NOT BE BROKEN.....

In summary , lets put it as thus ;

Question,,…. WHAT MAKES MEN RISE AND FALL?

Answer …......THE MIND

With the above puzzle , I went deeper to discover and rediscover again that both researches has proven beyond every reasonable doubt by both scientists   and philosophers that the mind is the seat of wisdom and as such   the most   attacked ,over continuous manipulated and target of the demonic kingdom and also the first contact of man and divinity. That is,   every spiritual conquest starts and ends in the MIND ,,, And that there is a continual war in the mind as regards to who takes the ownership of the   territory and as you , you can not act above your mind or thinking capacity and you know that every picture or imagination that is exhibited or is hoping for due manifestation is always a product of the MIND ,,,

Romans 12:1, KJV: "I beseech you therefore, brethren, by the mercies of God, that ye present your bodies a living sacrifice, holy, acceptable unto God, which is your reasonable service." ...
Romans 12:1, NLT: "And so, dear brothers and sisters, I plead with you to give your bodies to God because of all he has done for you.

1 John 3 vs 3 " All who have this hope in him purify themselves, just as he is pure."

Proverbs 23 vs 7 " For as he thinketh in his heart, so is he: Eat and drink, saith he to thee; but his heart is not with thee"

 Proverbs 4 vs 23 "Above all else, guard your heart, for everything you do flows from it.."

Lets take a pause now and explore some thinking capacity of winners and losers

From interviewing hundreds of Olympic winning athletes, they all answered that 90% of their game is MENTAL.

How much time do they spend on training mental part of the game? Usually answer is the same: very little or less than 10%.

What separates winners from others is mainly the way they THINK.

When athletes have mindset that they EXPECT to perform well, winning is automatically an option.   For others, hope is their mindset.

Desired outcome needs to be CONCRETE in your mind.

Process is primary.   Think about executing mental and physical processes, NOT about winning.   Thinking about winning can pull thoughts away from process but there is Need to think about PROCESS.

For business: Think about how you improve your mental and business processes, rather than making a certain amount of money.

"One thing is certain however, your worth as a person is not equal to your score this day but your mental daily developments "

For business purpose ,   Self worth is not equal to net worth" So, should we be concerned at all about winning? Certainly. And the best focus, in my view, is on a winning performance, not on finishing on top. I suggest that your goal   should be   set to have a winning performance on the day of competition instead of goal setting to win the competition. What is the difference you may ask? If your goal set is   to have a winning performance you will always be process-oriented and not outcome-oriented. You will be much less likely to over-try in the competition because you are always focused on the next step and not counting your score."

Principles of Mental Management

#1 – Your conscious mind can only focus on one thing at a time.

At any point in time you are either picturing something that will help you or hurt you.

If you are focused on leader board (business: money) then your performance will suffer.   If you focus on performing well for the shot (business: execution) then you maximize chance for success.

Take control of your thoughts so that they help you.

#2 – What you say is not important.   What you cause yourself or others to PICTURE is crucial.

#3 – The subconscious mind is the source of all mental power.

#4 – The self image moves you to do whatever the conscious mind is picturing.

"I realize that my self-image is moving me to perform what I am consciously picturing. I control what I picture and I only picture what I want to see happen"

#5 – Self image and performance are always equal.   To change your performance you must first change your self image.

The upper and lower limits of our comfort zone is defined by our self image.   If we perform below this zone, self-image will help us move back into the zone.   If we start performing above this zone, self-image will pull us down.   Change the zone to change performance.

If you believe that it is "like you" to earn $100,000 per year, you will trend towards that.

If your self-image is that it is "like you" to earn $10,000,000 per year, you will trend towards that.

#6 – You can replace the self image you have with the self image you want.

#7 – Principle of reinforcement.

The more we think about, talk about and write about something happening, we improve the probability of that thing happening.

We influence one another. All these principles are not just related to ourselves but also to our team mates.

Talk about your good shots. Will improve probability of good shots in future.

Write down goals.   Won't guarantee outcome, but helps build self image needed to attain the goal.

Be careful not to complain! This is negative reinforcement.

Do not reinforce a bad shot by getting angry.

Don't reinforce a bad day at the office by complaining to your spouse.

Instead, remember something that you did well during the day and focus on that instead.

Fill your thoughts only with the best performances.   This is like my journaling – "What went well and why".   Focus on positive to reinforce those outcomes, build self-image.

"Positive Prediction" – Reinforcement in advance. Compliment given in advance of future action.

GOAL SETTING

Most goal setting systems are flawed, because focus on outcome. The focus is often on score or winning competition.   Should set goals on the process of getting a score that can win the competition. When you focus on improving performance you are dealing with something in your control.   Outcome is not in your control.

E.g. you can control how many days per week you train. Can control the competitions you enter. Can choose how you train.

ONLY SET GOALS ON THINGS THAT YOU CAN CONTROL!

Keep your focus on YOU not on your competitors.

Pitfalls.   People equate worth as a person on whether they reach goal or not.

Step 1. Determine a goal worth trading your life for.

Step 2. Decide when you want it.

Putting a time limit help formulate plan to achieve goals.

Step 3.   List the pay value. WHY do you want the goal?

Step 4.   Evaluate obstacles in your way. What habits and attitudes do you need to change in order to achieve your goals?

Step 5.   What is the plan to get your goal?

Prepare a written plan to overcome each obstacle.

Step 6.   Evaluate Plan.

Step 7.   Schedule Plan.

Step 8. Start now.

Step 9. Prior to reaching goal, always set a new one to take its place.

REHEARSAL

Principle of Mental Management #8 – The self-image cannot tell the difference between what is real and what is vividly imagined.

Rehearsal relates to seeing and feeling desired results in the mind.

There is no one perfect way to do it. It is individual. For some blurry, for some vivid.   Can do it in seconds or minutes.

Do not wait until you feel totally prepared for competing. **Perfection is the purest form of procrastination.**

Praise in public, correct in private.   Public praise raises self image. Praise twice as much as you correct.   By praising you are building.

Mistakes hint;

Focus should be on learning from failure, not thinking about it.

- Use much more praise – build up team mates.   2x praise vs correction.   Praise in public, correct only in private.
- In business retrospectives – try using focus just on what went well?
- "Train with people who are better than you" – join high level mastermind.
- In journal write down my goals every day for business, social, relationships and any other critical areas of my life.
- Determine a key focus in my life.   Use mental rehearsal. Devote regular time per day (5 minutes) for this.

- Write down this key focus (directive affirmation) and put in prominent areas around work / home. Read and visualize multiple times per day.

Chapter 2

POSITIVE THINKING - NEGATIVE THINKING - RIGHT THINKING

The starting point of making permanent and lasting changes in your life begins with understanding the difference between "positive" thinking, "negative" thinking and "right" thinking. Think of the person who sits down to play the piano. As he plays, there is no harmony, no balance and no real tune because he keeps hitting all the wrong notes. The player eventually gets fed up with the disharmony, lack of pleasure and lack of enjoyment in his music and decides to go a teacher. The teacher says, "You have the ability to play, but you need to understand music." Each one of us has the ability to play the game of life with balance, harmony and joy, but we need to know the rules and the principles. Life works according to principle and physical law. If it didn't, you couldn't fly an airplane, because there would be no gravity, there would be no such thing as electricity, and one-plus-one would not equal two. The laws of the universe are totally dependable. Universal law is not only dependable, but also unchangeable. You can depend on it, and it will work every time. In essence, the universe will never let you down. It doesn't care how old you are, how young you are, how short, how fat, how skinny, your religion, your nationality or whether you are a male or a female. The Power, the Force, or   the Energy is neutral, and we direct it through our own ideas and beliefs. 8 Your Word is Law What we are saying is that your word is the law in the universe. But you need to know these laws. Without an understanding of the laws, through ignorance, you cannot create what you want. The fundamental law to which all other laws conform is the Law of Cause and Effect. The Law of Cause and Effect says that the effect or result of any situation must be equal to the cause. The cause is always an idea or   belief. Another way of describing the Law of Cause and Effect

is the example of sowing and reaping, or action and reaction. Or, put in a modern-day context - My ideas are created into my results. The Law of Cause and Effect is impersonal, just like sunshine. If you are standing in the sun, you receive the warmth and healing benefits of the sun's rays. If you are standing in the shade, it seems like the sun isn't shining on you. But who moved you into the shade? Who moved you into the darkness? The truth is we are in darkness because of our ignorance. The Problem of Ignorance I repeat, the Law of Cause and Effect is impersonal. This is why we can see so many people who are basically good have so many problems and disasters in their lives. Somewhere in their life that person has misused or misunderstood the law. It doesn't mean the he or she is bad. It doesn't mean the he or she isn't a loving person. It means that through ignorance or misunderstanding, that person has misused the law. This can be applied to any natural law. For instance, aerodynamics or gravity will not kill you, but a misunderstanding of its function will, even if you are a kind, loving, positive person. 9 The universe is like a river. The river keeps on flowing. It doesn't care whether you are happy or sad, good or bad; it just keeps flowing. Some people go down to the river and they cry. Some people go down to the river and they are happy, but the river doesn't care; it just keeps flowing. We can use it and enjoy it, or we can jump in and drown. The river just keeps flowing because it is impersonal. And so it is with the universe. The universe that we live in can support us or destroy us. It's our interpretation and use of the laws that determine our effects or results. We can only receive what our minds are capable of accepting. We can go to the river of life with a teaspoon, and someone else may go with a cup. Someone else may go with a bucket, and yet another person may go with a barrel. But the abundance of the river is always there and waiting. Our consciousness, our ideas, our frame of reference and our belief system determine whether we go to the river of life with a teaspoon, a cup, a bucket or a barrel. If we are impoverished in our thinking and have gone to the river of life with only a teaspoon, we may curse the little we have in our teaspoon. We may curse others who have more than we do. But remember, - whatever we curse will curse us. The river is there, and it's overflowing with abundance. We can come to the river of life with a teaspoon, a bucket or a barrel anytime we want to. What we take from the river of life is up to us. The only limitation is in our mind. The truth is we can have anything we want if we'll give up the belief that we can't have it. It's as   simple as that. 10 Beliefs Become Limitations All our experiences have led us to believe certain things about ourselves. Whether these beliefs are true or not really doesn't matter because if we accept them as true, then they are true for us. If we speak our word long enough, it becomes law in the universe. Pronounce your limitations vigorously enough and they're yours. Whether your beliefs are true or totally insane, if you accept them, then that's what your life will be about. Once we have accepted an idea, it's and idea whose time has come and there is nothing that can stop it. If we have accepted an idea of lack and limitation, it is an idea whose time has come for us.

There is nothing that we can do about it except to change our mind. If you plant a seed, it is going to grow. If you plant a tomato, you will have a tomato. The tomato won't change its mind and become a cucumber because it thinks a cucumber is better for you. The soil will give you tomatoes as long as you keep planting them, even if you are allergic to tomatoes. Look at the beliefs that form the groundwork of your life. We are full of beliefs that we have collected over the years - attitudes, ideas, opinions and conditioning. And we are so full of what we know that when challenged, we dig in our heels and often think, "Don't tell me anything new. I have my beliefs together and how dare you try to change them. This is what I've based my whole life on. Now you are telling me I could be wrong. I don't want to hear that." So we live with a set of beliefs called religion, a set of beliefs called politics, a set of beliefs about ourselves, a set of beliefs about the kind of people that we like or don't like and a set of beliefs about everything else. Many of the things that we believe - garnered from past experience, groups of people and individuals - are not true, but they are 11 the things that we have imagined to be true out of our need to survive. Because the will to survive and the desire for certainty are strong, we create rules about the nature of life and how it unfolds, and these rules become beliefs. Unfortunately those beliefs can also become limitations. Break Through Mistaken Beliefs The fact of the matter is we can only be successful to the degree that we are willing to shed our mistaken beliefs. When we experience sickness, failure, or lack, it is often because of the limitations in our own mind. The sad thing is that, even though we know our lives aren't working in certain areas, we are still afraid to change. We are locked into our comfort zone, no matter how self-destructive it may be. Yet, the only way to get out of our comfort zone and to be free of our problems and limitations is to get uncomfortable. We can only experience freedom in direct proportion to the amount of truth that we are willing to accept without running way. We must stop kidding ourselves, stop blaming others, and stop avoiding unpleasant decisions and start facing the truth that we may have accepted unworkable beliefs that are the direct cause of the events in our lives. It is not a question of going from negative thinking to positive thinking. It is a matter of moving toward "right thinking", which means moving toward knowing the absolute truth about who we are and our relationship to life. Right thinking, which is based in Truth and not illusion is the foundation that determines the solidity of all other thinking. Positive thinking and negative thinking are both filtered through our belief 12 system. Right thinking comes from being aware of the truth or the reality of any situation. Knowing the Truth Sets You Free Always seek to know the truth about any situation in which you are involved.

Look behind your present belief system and ask your Higher Self "What is the truth about this?" Your Higher Self will always reveal the truth to you if you are ready to hear it. When

     THE POWER OF POSITIVE MIND

you act upon that truth, you are using right thinking. It's not a matter of being positive or negative, but of simply being yourself. And when you are yourself, which means you are allowing your Higher Self to reveal the truth, every situation you are involved in will resolve itself perfectly. This might sound magical, but it is only the Law of Cause and Effect in action. The Starting Point of Success The aim of all great teachers since the beginning of time was to awaken us to the fact that we create our own reality. More importantly, that we are responsible for everything that happens in our lives. This includes the good, the bad and the ugly. If we believe that someone or something outside of ourselves is the cause of our problem we will always look outside of ourselves for the solution. In order to find the true answers to our problems, we must begin by looking at ourselves in a new way, which will cause us to see people and events in a new way. The outer world is in many ways a reproduction of our inner world. You must realize this. How many troubled people do you know who have not given the slightest attention to this fact? No amount of determination, no amount of willpower, inspiration or motivation will solve our problems if we look outside of ourselves for the answer. 13 The Law of Attraction Everything comes to us by the most elemental law of physics – LIKE ATTRACTS LIKE! This is called the Law of Attraction. The Law of Attraction, like all natural laws, operates with mathematical exactitude. It is impartial and impersonal, which means it works when you want it to and when you don't want it to. It has nothing to do with your personality, your religious beliefs, being a "good" or a "bad" person or anything else. No one lives beyond this Law. It is an irrefutable law as real as the Law of Gravity. Before the Law of Gravity was identified nobody knew it existed, and yet everyone was still affected by   it. Such is the case with the Law of Attraction. Most people are unaware of the mechanics of how it works and yet everyone is still affected by it. You don't need to know the mechanics of how the Law of Gravity works to keep yourself from floating off into space. You also do not need to know the mechanics of how the Law of Attraction works for it to function in your life. You may not have realized it until now, but everything you experience in your life is invited, attracted and created by you. There are no exceptions. That may not be good news if your life is not going the way you want it to. And since most of us are not too happy with what we have created in our lives, we have become highly gifted masters at attracting an overabundance of circumstances that we would rather not have. 14 The mind attracts whatever is familiar to itself. The frightened mind attracts frightening experiences. A confused mind attracts more confusion. The abundant mind attracts more abundance. Since we attract what we think about, it makes good sense to become aware of the subconscious thought patterns that control our lives. You Are Always "Right" The primary function of the subconscious mind is to follow the instructions of the conscious mind. It does this by "proving" that whatever the conscious mind believes is true. In other words, the job of the subconscious mind is to prove the conscious mind is always "right." So, if you consciously believe that you can't be, do, or have something, the subconscious will create the circumstances and find the people to prove that you are "right." The subconscious functions like the automatic pilot of an airplane. If the autopilot is set to go east, you can manually override the controls and go north. But as soon as you let go, the automatic pilot, which has been programmed to go east will control the plane, and you will fly east. Your subconscious does not change the reality of the world around you. It just filters the information that you present to it in order to support your beliefs or the picture that you hold in your mind. For example; if you believe that business is bad, or that there are no new opportunities for your business, your subconscious will ignore new opportunities to improve your business. Instead, it will only point out problems that support your belief that things are bad, or that there are no new opportunities. 15 Your subconscious cannot think for itself. It will draw to you only those things that are consistent with your deepest inner beliefs, nothing more, nothing less. If you do not know this as a truth, and do not realize that you create your reality out of your ideas, you will feel powerless to change your life for the better. Instead you will feel that you are the victim of people, circumstances and conditions. If you accept yourself as powerless you will look to something or someone outside of yourself to fulfill your desires. When you come to the understanding that everything that you want can be created through your mind, through the use of right thinking, which is simply clear thinking, you come to the realization that only you can give yourself what you want.

Trusting Your Creative Power To create what you want, you have to trust the Power within you. Now, when you are told to trust the Power within you, immediately you could say: "Look at the starvation. Look at the sickness, the war and the crime in the world. You are telling me to trust the Power? If this Power existed, why would it allow this to happen?" Well, the truth is, it doesn't allow anything to happen. Remember, we said the Power is neutral. It is simply the Power of Creation. It is the impersonal force of life. We can use this Power, or Life Force, to create anything that we want in our lives. Even if we choose from ignorance, it doesn't matter. It will support us in our ignorance until we learn from it. The effect will always be equal to the cause. If we're in a ditch, it means that the Power is supporting us in being in a ditch. If our life is immensely successful, it means that the Power supports us in our success. It all comes out of our ideas. 16 Thought Directs Power We said earlier that our ideas are created into our results. To put it another way, it is done unto you as you believe, not as you want, but as you believe. There is a vast difference between the two. When you think - the universe moves. This means that when you put an idea out into the universe, people, places and things come into your life to fulfill that idea. When we think, we actually cause things to happen. Look at what this Power has done in the universe. Look all around you and see all the marvelous creations, infinite in number. The best news of all is that same Power is within you. And, the more open, responsive and receptive you are to this Power the more fulfilling and magnificent your life will be. If this is true, then how does the Power work? You and I are indirect users of the power. Let me explain. When you started your car today, what did you have to do? Well, you had to turn your key, which turned a small starting motor, which in turn started the engine. The starter motor was powered by electricity. Now, what was the direct source of that electricity? Was it the battery? No, it wasn't. A battery is not an independent source. It has to be charged up.

Your Higher Self is essentially a battery within that receives its' Source of power or energy from the universe. It then stores that power for you to use for the purpose of creation. In science there is a formula known as Ohm's Law, which states that C equals E divided by R ($C=E/R$). C equals the amount of electrical energy that is available for your appliance at the place where you're going to plug it in. For example, C equals the amount of electricity to run your toaster. The power to run the appliance is the result of E, which is the direct power source, divided by R, which is the resistance the power meets while getting there.

Now, suppose the main power line coming 17 into the building where you live is 750,000 volts, but it comes into your house at 110 to 220 volts to run your appliances. To do this, transformers are used on the power line to reduce the power coming into your house to make it safe for application. This is just like the Power available to you. You have the Ultimate Power of the universe available to you, but it also has Infinite Wisdom, which might be referred to as a transformer. While our Higher Self is plugged into the Ultimate Power of the universe, this Power also has enough wisdom to put some transformers in between to insulate it so we don't get too much before we are ready for it and burn ourselves out. Now, if you wanted to bring in more power, what

     THE POWER OF POSITIVE MIND

would you do? You would have to create less resistance, and you would have to change the wiring to accommodate the additional flow of power. How to Have More Power This Power is like the water in our earlier example in the sense that a larger container is needed to carry greater quantities. You cannot expect that just because your Higher Self is plugged into the Ultimate Power, Intelligence and Wisdom of the universe, that you can just turn it on, because if you did you would blow yourself right out. So in order to get our lives to work, and take greater advantage of this energy, we have to build a bigger channel for Creative Intelligence to flow through. To enlarge this channel we have to expand our consciousness. Expanding our consciousness involves expanding our ideas and beliefs regarding ourselves and our relationship to this Power. And as we do this, we begin to experience more of this Ultimate Power, and our ability to create greatly increases. 18 You and I are creative beings, and we always have the capacity to create more. In fact, we are always creating, consciously or unconsciously.

By knowing who we are and the process by which we can expand the power within, we can begin to move our creation from the unconscious to the conscious. When we create on the conscious level, we are able to make choices. When we create on the unconscious level we cannot make choices. We often hear about how we have the "power of choice", but that is not entirely accurate. It is misleading to say someone chooses a dysfunctional relationship, money problems, or any other negative situation in his or her life. Most of the time we are operating in the "default mode" which is based on our past conditioning. Choice implies being conscious. However, when you are unconscious, you cannot make conscious choices. You are operating in the "default mode" or on "automatic pilot". The default mode is the survival mode. This is where the mind takes control without us even being aware of what is happening.

Choice begins when you stop identifying with your conditioned patterns of the past. Until you reach that point, you are unconscious. This means you are compelled to think, feel and act in certain ways according to the conditioning of your mind. When we can make choices, we're no longer the victim of our unconscious reactions. If our unconscious negative thinking does not support what we want, rather than trying to eliminate it, all we have to do is center on 19 "right thinking". "Right thinking" is a thought pattern that is based on truth. Truth by its very nature must always be "right". There is No Growth Without Discontent Your Higher Self always knows what is best for you. All you need to do is to assert that you want something better than you have right now. Realize that there is no growth without discontent. While it is important to live in the present moment and accept "what is", it is also important to grow from where we are. Study your dissatisfaction very carefully because it will tell you something about yourself. Your life is an ever- changing canvas. What are you going to paint on it? Are you going to paint lack and limitation? Because if you do your canvas is going to reflect lack and limitation. Are You Chained to Your Limitations? Have you ever gone to the circus and noticed that the great big elephants are tied to a wooden stake with just a thin rope? Also the baby elephants have a big chain around their legs that is tied to a long metal stake that goes deep into the ground. This happens because the baby elephants must be chained up when they are very tiny to keep them from trying to get away. If the stake is driven far enough into the ground and the chain is strong enough, the baby elephant won't be able to budge. Eventually the day will come when the baby elephant stops tugging and never tries to pull away again. Someone then replaces the metal stake with a wooden one, because they know the elephant has been conditioned to believe that he cannot get away. By creating our own limitation through 20 our belief system, we do the very same thing. We become limited not by reality, but by reality as we perceive it to be. I once had a cat that seemed to believe that he couldn't jump onto high places, so he wouldn't even try. As the cat got older, he grew senile and simply forgot he didn't know how to jump. One day I came home and the cat was sitting on the highest shelf on the bookcase. He had knocked over all the books and art objects. You see, in the cat's senility he forgot what he couldn't do! What would happen if we became senile in a positive way? We would quite possibly forget all the things that we can't do and just do them. Understand the Rules of Life Understand that if your life does not work the way you want it to, it is because you have accepted false beliefs that keep you from being all that you can be. Unfortunately, the majority of people on this planet feel stuck. When we look at the world and see the suffering, misery and impoverishment, when we see so many well-intentioned people doing without, the world looks insane. We see people giving up, believing that they have to take from others in order to have anything for themselves. Rarely do we look within for the answer to this confusion. Rarely does the individual really look to see what the rules of life are. So what happens is that in our ignorance of ourselves and of life, we hassle, fight and strain to get what we want. And it ends up not working anyway.

Playing the Game of Life You see, life is a game. Some people play the game of struggle. Some people play the game of sickness. Some people play the game of poverty. Some people play the game of being right all the time. Some 21 people play the game of being late. But some people play the game of happiness, abundance and health. It just helps to understand that each individual plays a game that he or she sets up, and that no one game is necessarily better than another. If the game were   not bringing us some sort of a payoff, we'd stop playing. Look at your own life. Try to see the secret satisfaction that you get out of not being fully in charge of your life. What kind of secret satisfaction could there possibly be in feeling victimized? How could anyone enjoy feeling weak, or poor or inadequate? The answer is in the payoff or pay value. For example, if you play the weak game, others will have to love you, take care of you and protect you. It is the ultimate way to get attention. If you play the game of being undecided all the time and let other people decide for you, then you are protected from blame if you make a mistake. In other words, if you keep both hands tied behind you, then you can expect someone to take care of you. In playing the helpless routine, you are actually controlling others. The power of "powerless" people is remarkable. They are good at making others play the part that they have written for them.

Look at the value that you are getting out of your payoff. An example is being sick. Look at the value you get out of being sick. You may be saying, "That is insensitive and cruel. You don't know what I've been through." No, it's not cruel. It's crueler to deny it. What you are really saying is that your disease has more power than you do to decide your destiny. The question here is who is giving the illness such power? If you are experiencing illness, just take a look at it. Don't pass any judgment on yourself. Just let it tell you something. Know that no matter what is going on in your body, it begins in your mind. Illness is the body's reaction to your mind. Since your body is a feedback mechanism of your mind, it will always let you know what is going on in 22 your consciousness and an emotional level. Let your body be your teacher. It is interesting that in our society it is totally okay to spend $50,000 on a heart attack, but what would people say if you spent that amount of money on just having fun? They would think you were crazy, and they would probably resent you. It seems we have our priorities mixed up. Perhaps if we spent
$50,000 on having fun, we wouldn't have so many heart attacks! Think about it. Having pleasure is abnormal, but having pain in normal. Waiting Is a Trap Why are we waiting to be healthy, to be happy, to be alive, to be wealthy, to start a new business, to fall in love, to communicate, to clear up the relationships we are in? Waiting is a trap. We wait for interest rates to go down, for the economy to get better, for a person to change, for the holiday to pass before starting a diet. But there will always be a reason to wait. What If Help Doesn't Show Up? I knew a beautiful, intelligent young

woman who had everything to live for and yet tried to kill herself several times with alcohol and drugs. Do you know why? She always felt something was missing from her life. She didn't know she could create her life the way she wanted to.

Instead, she was waiting for someone to bring her happiness to her. But that person never showed up. This desire to have other people provide our happiness, or the belief that we can provide others' happiness, accounts for the endless procession of social schemes and organized drives for a better world. 23 Our major illusion is that we can build a society that functions on a higher psychological and spiritual level than our present level of awareness. Many people urge us to work for a better society or a better world. This is a great error. Since we cannot create anything higher than our own level of awareness, society as a whole doesn't get much better. Society's systems for social change only adds a new burden on top of an old burden. Our overwhelmed mind has no idea what to do with all the social schemes thrust upon us. But in our desperation to make things better, it forces us to try to make sense out of nonsense. The problem is that we trying to "right" the world's "wrongs" from the outside in. We attempt to reform the outside world by   forcing outer conditions to change. Unfortunately, this outside- in approach is doomed to failure because we are dealing with   the effect instead of the cause. Changing from the Inside Out We need to remind ourselves, and every individual on this planet, that we can and must change the world from the inside out. We have overwhelming proof that the outside-in approach does not work. The long-term solution to poverty, lack and limitation lies in our ability to turn our inner potential into reality. The only way we can truly heal the world is to heal ourselves first. This is not a new message, but I think we need to remind ourselves of who we are and what we are capable of. We need to take responsibility for everything that has happened to us. Through the law of attraction, we attract either consciously or unconsciously everything that happens to us. Whatever anyone has done to us, we have participated in it, and are at some level, responsible. In essence, there are no 24 victims, only volunteers. This is a hard pill to swallow, but unless we accept it we cannot change things for the better. We have become a culture of blamers. Yet, if you wrist watch shows the wrong time, what would you do about it? Would you ask your neighbor to set their watch according to yours, or would you correct your watch? Unfortunately, we do not make similar corrections when our lives are not working. Instead, we insist that reality should conform to our illusion. Starting Point of Success Your unlimited power lies in your ability to control your thoughts. A confused mind works in the direction of sickness, poverty, lack and limitation rather than in the direction of abundance, health and success. If we are not creating our lives the way we want them to be, we are creating from our unconscious. But since life is consciousness, the most important task we have is the development of the highest possible consciousness. We can do this by looking at the conditions of our lives and challenging our beliefs, even if our ego is threatened. Whenever we want something in our lives, we must let go of anything that is between what we believe and what we want. In your heart, you know exactly what you want. And if you will listen to your intuition, it will tell you. Your mind will sell you out, but your intuition never will. You intuition is your connection with the Ultimate Power. Learn to trust it. People can control you through your mind, but they can never control you through your intuition. We imagine we will lose something by following our intuition. But have you ever taken a look at what you have lost by not following your 25 intuition? Whatever your intuition is telling you is what you need to hear. As you learn to trust it   more and more, it will reveal exactly what you need to do at any given moment. Your life is important. It is important to you, and it is important to the rest of the people on this planet. I believe that every person on this planet arrived here with a mission.

If   you will listen to your intuition your purpose or your mission will be revealed to you

Chapter Three

CREAT VALUE MORE THAN VOLUME
THE TRUTH ABOUT YOU

If you want to take control of your life, it's important that you gain a basic understanding of who you are. Our self-image, which is the picture of ourselves that we hold in our minds, becomes the key to our lives. All our actions, feelings and behavior, and even our abilities, are consistent with this formed picture. We literally act out the kind of person that we think that we are. What we need to be aware of is that as long as we hold onto that picture, no amount of willpower, effort, determination or commitment will cause us to be any other way, because we're always going to act the way we see ourselves.

Not to be any other way, we must first look at how we form our self-image. Our Mental Blueprint From birth onward, we collect hundreds of ideas about ourselves as being good or bad, wise or stupid, confident or fearful and so on. Through repetition, these often false identities harden into our self-image. This self-image either allows us to be happy and successful or it tyrannizes our lives. Whether we realize it or not, within ourselves is a 26 mental blueprint. It's a picture of the way that we think that we are. This blueprint is exact and complete down to the last detail.

This summary or blueprint is our self-image. However, this blueprint is not who we are, but rather who we think we are. The circumstances or conditions that formed our self-image may have been totally erroneous or blown out of proportion, but as far as we are concerned they are true. Once we record this information, we do not question its validity. Most of the time we can't even consciously recall how or where we obtained this information. We just live as though it were true. Even if it's not true, we believe it's true. The Secret of the Ages The vast majority has missed the message that all the great teachers since the beginning of recorded history have tried to share with their fellow human beings. The secret of the ages, the one most incredible truth that very few realize, is that at the Being level, which we will call your Higher Self, you are spiritually whole, complete and perfect. Just as a drop of water has all the qualities of the ocean, you have all the qualities of the Creator within you. Science, philosophy and religion all teach in their own way that there's ultimately ONE Power in the universe, and that we're one with the Power, Energy, Force, or whatever you're comfortable with. You and I are individualized expressions of all the Power of the universe. This can be called your Higher Self. We can never destroy the Higher Self within us.

We can deny that it's there, we can try to hide from it, we can lie about it, but ultimately we cannot change the fact that it's who we are. What we need 27 to do is to recognize that it is who we are and learn how to channel it through our thoughts.

Who You Are and What You Do Is Not the Same We must understand the distinction between who we are and what we do. Who we are is spiritually perfect, but what we do is not always perfect. The gap between who we are and what we do is created through ignorance. When we don't know that we are spiritually perfect, it follows that our actions will be less than perfect. I'd like you to do something right now.

Just say to yourself. "I know that who I am is spiritually perfect." Now listen to the little voice in your head. It's probably saying, "Oh, no, I'm not." The affirmation of perfection seriously threatens your ego. Your ego immediately sends back the response, "What do you mean you're perfect? Come on now, take a good look at yourself. Look at the way you treat other people. Remember what you did yesterday? You're always complaining. How about the way you treat your mother, your father, your boss and your mate? How about the way you treat yourself? And remember that terrible thing you did back in 1986? How can you say you are spiritually perfect after that? Take a good look at yourself and stop this nonsense." Your Ego Is Trying To Trick You You see, your ego does not want you to take a good look at yourself. It wants you to take a bad

     THE POWER OF POSITIVE MIND

look at yourself. It wants you to identify with everything that you're not. It wants you to identify with your actions and feel guilty. It wants you to judge, condemn and blame yourself for not living up to the pictures and expectations of yourself and 28 others. You must recognize that your ego is trying to trick you. This is not the truth about you. The way out of this is to affirm your own perfection. It's not an ego trip to affirm your own perfection. It's an ego trip not to affirm your own perfection. Remember, the first and most essential step in changing your life, no matter what you want to be, do or have, is to realize your own perfection based upon the truth about you, that you are spiritually whole, complete and perfect. Neutralizing Your Ego The way to neutralize your ego is to love yourself unconditionally. Loving yourself doesn't bloat your ego.

Loving yourself actually neutralizes your ego, because your ego isn't about loving yourself. We need to understand that life is consciousness. This means that what we assume to be true will become real for us. Whatever we're conscious of, we will experience. In essence, we will experience in life what we're deeply convinced is so. This statement is important. We experience in life what we're deeply convinced is so. If our thought patterns say, "I cannot have this or that, I don't deserve this or that, I'm a bad person" and so on, we continue to create conditions that correspond to our ideas of evil, lack and limitation. The bottom line is this: If we cannot accept ourselves, that we're worthy and deserving, then we cannot accept that other people are worthy and deserving, and will therefore be in judgment of them. The solution is to develop unconditional love of ourselves and others. This is the only way that we can ever be free.

We must have 29 total acceptance of ourselves first and then others, knowing that, as we are spiritually perfect, so is everyone else. You Have Created Yourself In a very important way, you've created yourself whether you realize it or not. All the character traits, mannerisms, ways of talking, ways of walking, facial expressions, gestures and even ways of thinking and believing, you have borrowed, imitated or made your own. It may have been from a parent or other family members, a favorite teacher, a friend, or a character in a book or a movie. Maybe you borrowed from someone you didn't even like. It may have been from someone who made you feel uncomfortable or afraid. Imitating that person could have been a way of making you feel less afraid and a way of intimidating others.

Never Reject Yourself in Any Way It's important to take a look at the personality that you've created. Perhaps one of the reasons you keep yourself from doing this is because you've been an imitator. It's not uncommon to get hung up on this. It may help to understand that nobody can create a Self from scratch. Everyone has to do the same thing. Everybody chooses from what's available. Even though you may have built your personality through imitation, you're not a fraud. No one else has ever put together the exact same combination that you have. Don't forget there are only twelve notes in the musical scale, and yet many hundreds of thousands of unique and beautiful combinations are created. It's all a matter of how they are put together. 30 It doesn't make you any less of a unique person to have taken from others. The wonderful thing about this is that since you put it together from scratch, you can change it at any time you want to. You're never stuck. It's not a disaster to discover that you're not the person that you thought that you were. On the contrary, it's the beginning of the end of disaster. In order to change the experiences that are causing you pain and disharmony, it's necessary to begin with a clear understanding that you never help yourself by rejecting any part of yourself. We get into self-hatred because we set up picture of how we think we should be based on the conditioning from our family, peer groups, mate, religion, and the society that we live in. The sad part of this is that we'll never be able to live up to the pictures, images, models, standards or concepts of how we think we should be. It's a psychological dead-end. Freedom Begins with Self-Acceptance We've allowed our ego to trick us into believing that we're incompetent, inadequate, insecure, stupid, bad, evil and unworthy. All of this can be summed up as poor self-esteem and a poor self-image.

Until we make a conscious decision to change our thought patterns, we will continue to have poor self-esteem and a poor self-image. The first and most important thing in your life is self-acceptance, to love who you are - to be yourself. Only when you love yourself can you begin to love others. Many people say you should forget about yourself and love others first. Well, it doesn't work that way. The truth is, you must first accept yourself with all your mistakes - all of your so-called sins, all the times you looked like a fool, and all the times you've acted inappropriately. You must be able to stand before the entire world and 31 make no excuse for yourself. When you can do that, you're coming from a position of unconditional love. How you see yourself creates your behavior, and this behavior creates your environment or your results. When you attach your selfworth to your accomplishments or to your behavior, you're setting yourself up for disappointment. No matter how hard you try; someone is going to think you're not okay.

Remember this: you'll always be a failure in someone's eyes. You'll never win everyone over, sometimes not even a majority. Take a look at how much of your life is about winning approval and realize this important truth: You'll never get the approval you seek! You simply can't please everyone, so learn to please yourself and enjoy who you are. You Can't Fail as a Person It's worth repeating that who you are is spiritually perfect, but what you do is not always perfect. What you do may succeed or fail, but you can detach yourself from the results by remembering that you can never be a success or a failure based on what you have and what you do. There's no way that you can fail in life as a person. You're not set up that way. When you're into hating yourself for all the things that you've done or haven't done, or into hating other people for what they haven't given you, you're into suffering. Suffering is a way of putting yourself down. It's a way of being angry with yourself.

If you really get down to it, anger and suffering and lack of happiness in our lives comes from being disappointed in ourselves for not living up to some expectation that we have of ourselves, or that someone else has of us.

In working with people who have self-destructive behaviors, I have found that the major cause of their behavior is self-hatred. Their self-hatred stemmed from the fact they hadn't lived up to someone else's expectations. Most of us judge ourselves on the basis of what we have or don't have and what we've accomplished or what we haven't. We feel that when we are a failure, we've let others and ourselves down. When we don't come up to the expectations of our parents, employers, religion, friends or mate, we conclude that we're no good. This is known as self-judgment. When you're standing in judgment of yourself, you will judge yourself as bad. And as soon as you put yourself down for something that you have or haven't done, or something that did not work out, or for a situation where you disappointed someone else, you feel bad. Yet this type of judgment only serves to carve away at what little self-esteem you have. It never does any good; it only destroys. It's true that each one of us has things in our lives that we regret, but at some point we have to stop dwelling on the regret and move on. We have to learn the lesson and throw away the experience. We can never be for anyone as long as we are against ourselves.

To be against others is to be against ourselves. This is a spiritual and psychological truth. The most corrupt thing that we can do is to judge someone. To suppress another individual and take away another's aliveness is one of the most negative and self-destructive behaviors a person can have. Release Everyone Including Yourself What would happen if you had no regrets of the past? Try to image what would happen if you totally forgave everyone in your life 33 regardless of what they did to you? Hopefully you are beginning to see that to the degree that you cannot forgive - whether it be yourself or someone else - you perpetuate unhappiness, poverty, sickness, lack and limitation in you life. Many people don't want to forgive others. They say things like, "Why should I let them off the hook after what they did to me? The enemy is always someone we think can harm us or take something away from us, but the truth is no one can harm us. People harm us through ourselves. Actually they don't harm us at all. We give them instructions on how to treat us, and they just follow through. Make a decision to give up all resentment right now, because in the end it will eventually destroy you. "Yes," you say, "I agree with you, but you don't know my circumstances. They really hurt me. Maybe I'll give up my resentment

      THE POWER OF POSITIVE MIND

someday, but right now I can't let go." Understand that this mentality is more harmful and destructive to you than it is to the person that you resent. Turn your attention to this idea: You cannot be wealthy if you resent wealthy people. You cannot be successful if you resent successful people. You cannot be happy if you resent happy people. Whatever you resent is a statement of what you lack.

This also applies to healing. You cannot be healed if you have resentment towards anyone because resentment breaks down your immune system and literally cause your own sickness. Remember, whomever you resent is you, because we're all one. Rather than resent people who have what you don't have, or do what you cannot do, take the time to learn from these people. Let them become your teachers. Be with masters. Be with people who know how life works. Admire them, acknowledge them and support them in having 34 what they have. And as you do that, you actually support yourself in having what you want. If you study philosophy and religion, you will see that the values, morals and principles they teach are often rooted in the belief that something is better than something else. A is always better than B. Don't get caught in that trap. Forget about what other individuals or groups believe is "right" for you. Instead, realize you are connected to the same Source of Power and that you know what is best for you. Pleasing Others is A Psychological Dead-End About 700 years ago, a great teacher ripe with years and honors lay dying. His students and disciples asked if he was afraid to die. "Yes," he said, "I am afraid to meet my Maker." "But how can that be?" the students and disciples responded. "You have lived such an exemplary life. You led us out of the wilderness like Moses. You have judged between us wisely like Solomon." Softly he replied, "When I meet my Maker, He will not ask, 'Have you been like Moses or Solomon?' He will ask, 'Have you been yourself?' The story shows that throughout time, people have struggled to be themselves. Why are we still struggling? The struggle comes out of our need to please others. By assuming your own destiny, you're bound to get someone angry - your boss, your spouse, your parents, your children. At first assuming your own destiny can be a lonely process, and it may seem that everyone is against you. But the only image you must live up to is your own. The opinions of those who approve or disapprove are irrelevant. The decision to live your life is your own responsibility. The results of your own life are your own responsibility. Your action or 35 inaction becomes your own responsibility. Often other people will have values and beliefs that are in conflict with yours. And when they see you living in opposition to their values and beliefs, it can be very frightening for them because, in a way, it threatens their foundation. When a person is confronted with your beliefs, there's an inner battle that's waged, and the battle is, "Could they possibly be right? And if they are, that means I could be wrong." A person who knows who they are is not threatened by the beliefs of others. Those who are insecure and do not know who they are will always be frightened by anyone who directly or indirectly threatens their belief system. How Do You Treat Yourself? Let me ask you, Do you like yourself? Do you trust yourself? Do you keep promises that you make to yourself? Do you think that you're a good person? Are you yourself most of the time, or have you developed an act to cover up who you are? If you had a friend who treated you like you treat yourself, or talked to you the way that you talk to yourself, and broke commitments to you the way that you break commitments to yourself, do you think you'd keep him as a friend? Let's face it, you probably wouldn't want that type of person around. It's very important to take a look at the way we treat ourselves.

Most of the time we are our own worst enemy. We are afraid to meet our inner selves because we think we may not like what we see. I often hear people say, "I want to explore myself, but I'm afraid of what I'm going to find out about myself. I'm afraid of the strange creatures that I may find along the way or along the journey." Understand this clearly, it is absolutely impossible for the truth about yourself to cause fear. No matter how terrible the truth may be, it is 36 powerless in itself to either frighten or harm you. Fear is caused by resistance to the truth and by misunderstanding it. Start the Journey of Self-Discovery Start your journey of self-discovery at once. Nothing but good can come from it. The understanding of fear cures fear. Don't get hung up on the kind of person that you think that you are. Don't concern yourself with whether

     THE POWER OF POSITIVE MIND

you're better or worse than other people. Instead, try to know yourself as the kind of person that you are and the kind of person you would like to be. If you look at a half-finished house that is under construction, you don't condemn it for its unfinished condition. You don't say it's inferior to another house, nor are you concerned with its appearance. All you do is realize its need for additional work. Adopt this way of thinking toward yourself. Whatever your present condition, just realize the need for more construction. Be patient with yourself, but be firm toward the necessary work that needs to be done. Self-worth comes from Self. That's why it's not called "Other worth". If your worth comes from others, you will never be able love yourself. When you're an expert on yourself, you're an expert on everyone else. A conscious person knows himself. He knows his own nature, and therefore he knows everything about other people who have the same nature. Know yourself as you are, and you will know others as they are. Never be afraid to expose a weakness in yourself. Exposing a weakness is the beginning of strength. Remember - everything you learn about yourself is good news. No matter how difficult or surprising it 37 may be, it's always good news. Keep this in mind, especially in times when a new truth clashes with a belief that you know you must abandon but are reluctant to do so. A wise person is willing to give up a piece of coal in exchange for a diamond. Have the courage to do this and self change begins. You don't have to have permission from others to change your life. Don't ask, "Is this right for me to go against everything that I've been taught to believe?" Instead say, "Let me see how much intensity I can put into my search." Your own desire for personal freedom is the only search warrant you will every need. Take a Look At What You Are Denying Yourself If you're really going to learn the truth about you and live your life as you're capable of living, a lot of people aren't going to like it because they're not committed to the same path as you are. Are you going to deny yourself riches because others are poor? Are you going to deny yourself health because millions of people are sick? Take a good look at what you're denying yourself, and don't ever think of yourself as "wrong" for wanting what you want. As we move along the path of self-discovery, we're bound to make mistakes. Those so-called mistakes, faults, sins or errors are not you. Make sure you separate who you are from what you have and what you do.

You transcend what's happening in your life as you come to the realization that what's happening in your life is only temporary and will always be changing. It's important to understand that your Higher Self is changeless.

When you identify with your temporary nature, you take on the belief that what you have and what you do is the real you. It's possibly the biggest error that you can make in life. 38 To experience your own magnificence requires that you separate what you have and what you do from who you are. Learn to separate the performance from the performer, to become involved in what's happening in your life, but not to identify with its temporary nature. As you stand on the seashore and watch the ships sail by there is no problem as long as you simply stand there and watch them go by. It's only when you identify with the ships that you feel pain and suffering. If you say, "That's my ship," then you will grieve when it passes from your sight. If you say, "I must command that ship," then you will live in fear that someone else will become its captain. Likewise, by simply watching and observing our mistakes and unworkable behavior without judgment, we prevent harmful identification with our temporary mistakes, faults and errors. The Only Authority Figure Is Within Yourself As you start to question and look honestly at your life, you come to the point where you begin to realize that the only authority figure is within yourself. We look to other authorities to tell us what we're supposed to do, but the only person who will ever know what to do is ourselves. Have you ever wondered why certain people are conned by con artists? A con artist cannot con someone who is conscious. People have trouble understanding why others take advantage of them.

The reason they get taken advantage of is because they give their power away and they don't want to be responsible for their own lives. They don't want to make their own decisions so they allow others to do it for them. But understand this truth: If you allow others to do it for you, they'll do it to you. As long as you let others have responsibility for your life, they will control your destiny.   Why Do You Want To Change Your World? It's easy to say that others are to blame, but this type of thinking puts us further into bondage because we set limits on our freedom. Once again, straightening up our thinking involves separating what we have and what we do from who we are inside - separating the "doer" from the "deed". The secret is to live in this world but not let the world live in us. We want our boat in the water, but we don't want the water in our boat. When the water's in our boat, we start to sink, and we have to bail like crazy to stay afloat. The problem is we often find ourselves drowning in the water of physical effects that we've created in our lives. Once we're drowning we don't know any other way to deal with it except to fight it and try to change our circumstances. Before I go any further, let me ask you: "Why do you want to change your world?" Every time we attempt to change what ever is   going on around us, whether it be our business, our career, the government, members of our family, our mate or whatever, we're operating under of the illusion that these people and events are doing something to us. Actually, what we need to do is to change our experience in relation to them. People and events never do anything to us. They merely trigger feelings that are already within us. If we go back to the basic principle of life we understand that nothing happens in the world that we don't permit deep within our consciousness.

It's been said many ways that it is done unto you as you believe, and sometimes those beliefs are very deep. Whatever is going on within our heart is in fundamental alignment with our outside experiences, even though we may not be consciously aware of it. I know this principle is difficult to accept because there are 40 undoubtedly things in your life that you consciously do not want. However, the truth of the matter is, there's some deep inner need that you are satisfying. Imagine an unhappy person sitting at home stating, "I want to change my life." This person redecorates his house. Then he finds himself just as unhappy as before. So he redecorates several times, and he still feels no change in himself. Do you know people who believe that they can change their level of happiness by changing their exterior scenery? Where have they made a mistake?

Where can they correct themselves? If you will be totally honest with yourself and take a good look at what's going on in your life, you'll discover what is actually happening. Therefore it stands to reason that if we attempt and are successful in changing the outer effect but don't change the inner causation, we will only create the same experience again. If you no longer know what to do, this process of self-evaluation is a very good path to finding yourself. It will help you to understand that the mechanical thinking process cannot rise above its own limited level. If you're not sure what to do or if you have any anxiety, don't try to seek release from the anxiety. Just stay where you are and let it tell you something extraordinary, and it will. So the truth about you is that you're not what you have and you're not what you do. You are spiritually whole, complete and perfect, and your success and happiness in life will be in direct proportion to your ability to accept this truth about yourself.

Chapter Four

DO NOT WAKE UP TIRED

Ways to Combat Brain TIREDNESS.
- ShareYou might know all too well that feeling of constant exhaustion, tiredness and lethargy despite doing all the commonly prescribed self-care treatments.

You feel mentally tired.

Let's not deny exercise, getting enough sleep and clean eating are all important. However, you are doing all those things and are still feeling exhausted.

There is a great chance there are deeper mental and emotional issues your brain is constantly feeling under attack from and therefore is suffering from constant mental fatigue. It feels like you just can't seem to get a break and you are constantly running on the treadmill and cannot step off, even if you want to.

Doing a U-turn on this path can be tough but definitely not impossible. In fact, these life-changing mental strategies will not only help to relieve this constant mental tiredness but help you truly springboard to a new level of peak functioning you might not have ever experienced before.

1. Review your core values and ask yourself if you are operating in alignment with those.
One of the most common reasons people leave their jobs is because of their boss. In a survey of 7500 full-time employees, Gallup found 23% of respondents felt burnt out often or always whilst 44% reported feeling burnt out sometimes.[1]

You will be surprised to learn the burnout was not attributed to increased work performance or productivity but rather how the employees were managed. Unfair treatment at work, lack of role clarity, unmanageable workloads, lack of support from their manager and unreasonable time pressure were the top five factors correlated with respondents experiencing burnout.

If you are regularly struggling to have your core work values honored (e.g. trust, open communication, respect, collaboration), it is high time to look at having a conversation around this with your boss.

By discussing with your boss how being able to have these values met will better benefit them and the greater good of the organization, you create a win-win for all!

Get clear on what you will and won't tolerate. Listen to your gut on what is deeply and truly important. Getting clarity on this alone will give you greater awareness to be able to respond better when things happen that throw you mentally off-course. The awareness and new clarity will massively reduce that brain exhaustion!

2. Choose to set the mental tone of your day.
Which do you think is going to better influence having a mentally easier day?

- Starting the day getting up late, having breakfast of coffee laden with sugar whilst you listen to the tragedies of the world news on the television; OR
- Waking up earlier, doing five minutes of stretching to calm music, listening to an inspiring podcast that gives you ideas and solutions and having a nourishing breakfast, smoothie or juice?

Choose how you want your day to start. Make easy simple changes and practice sticking to them each day.

Even if you face a disaster first thing upon arriving at the office, your brain is already riding a relaxed wave that puts you in a clearer mindset to put out those fires than if you have already started the day in a stressed mental state.

Give yourself a head start!

3. Examine what drains your energy and make necessary changes.
When your colleague or partner is expressing anger, fear, sadness, frustration and other similar emotions coupled with solution-focused

discussion, you feel purposeful and energetically uplifted just supporting them.

However, not being able to get a word in when they talk at you, whine, complain and blame the world around them for their misfortunes will drain energy from you and fry your brain. That loss of energy costs you greatly!

It can be a great idea to start training those friends, family or colleagues that when they need to download with you (with you, not on you) there are conditions. Those conditions might be whingeing and complaining for twenty minutes freely but then the focus needs to be about looking at solutions.

If you get sprung unexpectedly by a whingeing phone call, gently inquire what they are calling about first before launching into the meat of the conversation. If you can sense it is going to be a mentally heavy conversation, state you have a limited time available. Make sure you have a get-out clause ready!

Your mental state deserves to be preserved and protected. Stop making yourself available as a mental, emotional punching bag at the leisure of anyone who does not have the same capacity for mental and emotional regulation as you. They are not your problem to fix.

Give periodic support but empower them to become their own change agents by directing them to additional sources of support.

4. Get good at relaxing on cue, not on demand.
Stress deactivates your attention and concentration capacity and your ability to think creatively diminishes.

When you are anxious, you deplete your brain's ability to think about what it is you really want and what is important to you. When your brain is in a relaxed state, dopamine levels are increased freeing up mental and emotional space. Only then can you truly choose what you want to turn your attention and energy to.

    THE POWER OF POSITIVE MIND

Choose wisely! By relaxing your mind first and then focusing on positively reinforcing thoughts and ideas you greatly reduce your mental (and physical) fatigue.

<u>Practicing mindfulness</u> first and then choosing wisely what you want to focus on is like wiping your glass lenses clean before trying to see clearly.

Feeling Stuck in the Middle of a Challenge?
> Here's your guide to getting unstuck and regaining motivation!

DownlIncrease practicing having a relaxed brain as your default state as opposed to a reactive after-thought. Because you have momentarily slowed down, you will be able to speed up.

5. Develop creative sources of internal motivation.
Long-term gratification is a noble thought. The problem is your brain naturally looks to steer you in directions which bring you immediate satisfaction, that keeps you safe and happy now.

Search for and/or create steps in your journey that ignite a positive emotional shift for you in as many ways as possible. Be creative with this. Instead of allowing the guilty feeling of leaving the office with that project still incomplete, practice thinking more about your children's and partner's radiant faces surprised and delighted to see you home earlier than usual.

You get to feel better about yourself when you invest in quality relationships. Let them re-nourish you so you can dive back into that project refreshed and with better focus tomorrow.

6. Reframing your current perspective can greatly shift and lift mental fatigue.
Stating to yourself that you are overwhelmed can't manage and that you are burnt out can become a dangerous self-fulfilling prophecy. Practice a thought-stopping word such as 'shift' to help stop the wheels turning in that downward spiral direction. From there, see if you can recognize that

in those moments you are feeling overwhelmed but you are not actually stuck in being overwhelmed.

You are feeling you can't manage and feeling burnt out but you actually are not those labels. You merely feel those things in your moments of emergency.

Feelings are transient. According to Dr. Joan Rosenberg, the most heightened part of our intense emotions lasts for about ninety seconds. After that, the energy of what we are feeling starts to subside if we don't fight what we are feeling.[2]

Embrace that and let the sting of those feelings run their course. As they subside, you will mentally feel more relaxed and your brain will have a greater capacity to shift into a new gear.

7. Reduce, minimize or eliminate your exposure to prolonged stressors or stressful periods.
This can be much harder to put into practice. You might gradually need to look at the people, activities, your work and ways you operate in your relationships and friendships to see what stressors you are exposing yourself to and how often.

Working with a coach or mentor – someone who is completely non-biased in your assessment – can greatly help to really map out where your mental tiredness is truly exacerbated. Some friendships may need to end. You may need to explore flexible work options with your boss.

The journey will be easier when you develop and gradually work through a hierarchy of gradual change.

8. Increase qualified support networks and resources.
Most would think that asking for help and assistance automatically reduces your mental tiredness. However, getting advice and help from people who are not qualified or biased about how you can overcome your challenges can plummet your mental tiredness further and make matters worse.

Start asking yourself three questions:

1. What sort of support, guidance and help do I need?
2. Where are the places I know where to get that help?
3. What qualifies this person or resource to be able to provide me with that help?
4. Are they coming from a position that unconditionally supports me or are they projecting their own views and expectations upon me?

It is nonsensical to ask someone who has no business ownership experience – nor run a successful business – how to run a business. The same goes for any area of our life, professional or personal. Yet, we often do this.

The more we make unsuitable choices of where we get our advice, information and guidance from, we will continue to be mentally tired. We then sustain unhelpful behaviors which keep us stuck and safe.

Be more discerning about who and where you get your advice and guidance from, gain better clarity about the way forward and lift another level of that festering fatigue!

9. Build in pause time.
Positive and constructive day-dreaming allows you to mentally breathe. According to Dr. Srini Pillay, Assistant Professor of Psychiatry at Harvard Medical School, we daydream for approximately 46.9% of the day!

We may as well take advantage of this fact and direct it using positive constructive day-dreaming.[3] You can biologically change your brain by carefully constructing the imagery that you tell your brain to create.

Focus on overcoming your challenges and see yourself in the process of actually doing what is required. Do this at the same time as a low-concentration activity such as meandering-type walking (not power walking in the gym) and double your impact. Overcome your brain exhaustion by directing imagined focus on what you want and where you want to go.

  THE POWER OF POSITIVE MIND

Peta Ellis , CEO of River City Labs which fosters some of Australia's newest and most innovative businesses, is a serial start-up founder who swears by having 'headspace for Peta'. Between 4:00 am and 5:00 am, Peta speaks to no one, does gentle exercise and listens to music. Her days are filled with talking with people constantly so she does not negotiate on having this time for herself.

At moments throughout the day, she schedules in non-interrupted fifteen-minute pockets to reflect on how she is feeling, self-monitor and reflect on how she is progressing and also what she needs to do next.

How to Go from Overwhelmed to Motivated?
Find Out Now

Scheduled pauses are one of her most powerful assets to maintaining such a strong entrepreneurial drive.

10. Gradually reduce procrastination on things that really need active attention.

The more you resist, the more it persists. The reality is that the longer important things are left unattended, the more detrimental the negative consequences can become. Rumination then becomes layered with greater feelings of guilt, disappointment and pressure all of which add to your brain feeling exhaustion.

If you are going to procrastinate, do it properly!

Give yourself full permission to do menial administration tasks and unproductive email sorting but set a time limit on it. Then set a limited time period devoted to the activity you MUST attend to.

Don't necessarily aim for completion if that puts extra psychological pressure on your mindset. Simply aim to dedicate good effort for that period of time.

Throughout her life's work of research on mindset, Stanford University Professor of Psychology Dr. Carol Dweck explains that when we place

emphasis on dedicating quality effort as opposed to ensuring a certain
outcome, completing the job becomes and feels easier. You then set your
next dedicated procrastination time to be slightly shorter…and shorter
again.[4]

Before you know it, you will become more productive with less effort
and your mental space will become clearer.

11. Choose to stimulate your mind with energizing information.
If you have career challenges which are not easily or immediately
solvable, spending all your waking hours watching television shows such
as Jerry Springer are going to add to your feeling mentally tired.

Invest a little time to strategically choose <u>literature</u>, <u>podcasts</u> and being
around people that help you work through your current challenges.
Whilst driving, listen to an audio book with content that helps you learn
how to work through your problems or talk with your passenger about
ideas and solutions which energize and increase your motivation to
tackle your day ahead.

However, be careful of taking this to the extreme. Becoming a serial
course junkie and having a podcast to fill up every other second you are
not working will fry your brain.

Your body's muscles become stronger whilst repairing on the rest days
after you have completed a weights session at the gym. In similar
fashion, your mind becomes stronger when you choose helpful
energizing information to feed it but you must allow rest time for your
mind to process it to gain the full benefit.

Chapter Five

CHANGE IS POWERFUL

Why is it so hard to make lasting changes in our companies, in our communities, and in our own lives? The primary obstacle is a conflict that's built into our brains, say Chip and Dan Heath, authors of the critically acclaimed bestseller Made to Stick. Psychologists have discovered that our minds are ruled by two different systems-the rational mind and the emotional mind-that compete for control. The rational mind wants a great beach body; the emotional mind wants that Oreo cookie. The rational mind wants to change something at work; the emotional mind loves the comfort of the existing routine. This tension can doom a change effort-but if it is overcome, change can come quickly. In Switch, the Heaths show how everyday people---employees and managers, parents and nurses-have united both minds and, as a result, achieved dramatic results: • The lowly medical interns who managed to defeat an entrenched, decades-old medical practice that was endangering patients • The home-organizing guru who developed a simple technique for overcoming the dread of housekeeping • The manager who transformed a lackadaisical customer-support team into service zealots by removing a standard tool of customer service   In a compelling, story-driven narrative, the Heaths bring together decades of counter intuitive research in psychology, sociology, and other fields to shed new light on how we can   effect trans formative change. Switch shows that successful changes follow a pattern, a pattern you can use to make the changes that matter to you, whether your interest is in changing the world or changing your waistline.

One Saturday in 2000, some unsuspecting moviegoers showed up at a suburban theater in Chicago to catch a 1 :05 p.m. matinee of Mel Gibson's action flick Payback. They were handed a soft drink and a free bucket of popcorn and were asked to stick around after the movie to answer a few questions about the concession stand. These movie fans were unwitting participants in a study of irrational eating behavior. There was something unusual about the popcorn they received. It was wretched. In fact, it had been carefully engineered to be wretched. It had been popped five days earlier and was so stale that it squeaked when you ate it. One moviegoer later compared it to Styrofoam packing peanuts, and two others, forgetting that they'd received the popcorn for free, demanded their money back. Some of them got their free popcorn in a medium-size bucket,

Three surprises that Change and others got a large bucket-the sort of huge tub that looks like it might once have been an above-ground swimming pool. Every person got a bucket so there was   no need to share. The researchers responsible for the study were interested in a simple question: Would the people with bigger buckets eat more? Both buckets were so big that none of the moviegoers could finish their individual portions. So the actual research question was a bit more specific: Would somebody with a larger inexhaustible supply of popcorn eat more than someone with a smaller inexhaustible supply? The sneaky researchers weighed the buckets before and after the movie, so they were able to measure precisely how much popcorn each person ate. The results were stunning: People with the large buckets ate 53 percent more popcorn than people with the medium size. That's the equivalent of 173 more calories and approximately 21 extra hand-dips into the bucket. Brian Wansink, the author of the study, runs the Food and Brand Lab at Cornell University, and he described the results in his book Mindless Eating: "We've run other popcorn studies, and the results were always the same, however we tweaked the details.

It didn't matter if our moviegoers were in Pennsylvania, Illinois, or Iowa, and it didn't matter what kind of movie was showing; all of our popcorn studies led to the same conclusion. People eat more when you give them a bigger container. Period." No other theory explains the behavior. These people weren't eating for pleasure. (The popcorn was so stale it squeaked!) They weren't driven by a desire to finish their portion. (Both buckets were too big to finish.) It didn't matter whether they were hungry or full. The equation is unyielding: Bigger container = more eating. Best of all, people refused to believe the results. After the movie, the researchers told the moviegoers about the two bucket sizes and the findings of their past research. The researchers asked, ' Do you think you ate more because of the larger size? The majority scoffed at the idea, saying, "Things like that don't trick me," or, "I'm pretty good at knowing when I'm full." Whoops. 2. Imagine that someone showed you the data from the popcorn eating study but didn't mention the bucket sizes. On your data summary, you could quickly scan the results and see how much popcorn different people ate-some people ate a little, some ate a lot, and some seemed to be testing the physical limits of the human stomach. Armed with a data set like that, you would find it easy to jump to conclusions. Some people are Reasonable Snackers, and others are Big Gluttons. A public-health expert, studying that data alongside you, would likely get very worried about the Gluttons. "We need to motivate these people to adopt healthier snacking behaviors! Let's find ways to show them the health hazards of eating so much! But wait a second. If you want people to eat less popcorn, the solution is pretty simple: Give them smaller buckets. You don't have to worry about their knowledge or their attitudes. You can see how easy it would be to turn an easy change problem (shrinking people's buckets) into a hard change problem (convincing people to think differently). And that's the first surprise about change: What looks like a people problem is often a situation problem.

This is a chapter to help you change things. We consider change at every level-individual, organizational, and societal. Maybe these three Surprises about change wants to help your brother beat his gambling addiction. Maybe you need your team at work to act more frugally because of market conditions. Maybe you wish more of your neighbors would bike to work. Usually these topics are treated separately-there is "change management" advice for executives and "self-help" advice for individuals and "change the world" advice for activists. That's a shame, because all change efforts have something in common: For anything to change, someone has to start acting differently. Your brother has got to stay out of the casino; your employees have got to start booking coach fares. Ultimately, all change efforts boil down to the same mission: Can you get people to start behaving in a new way? We know what you're thinking-people resist change. But it's not quite that easy. Babies are born every day to parents who, inexplicably welcome the change.

Think about the sheer magnitude of that change! Would anyone agree to work for a boss who'd wake you up twice a night, screaming, for trivial administrative duties? (And what if, every time you wore a new piece of clothing, the boss spit up on it?) Yet people don't resist this massive change-they volunteer for it. In our lives, we embrace lots of big changes-not only babies, but marriages and new homes and new technologies and new job duties.

Meanwhile, other behaviors are maddeningly intractable. Smokers keep smoking and kids grow fatter and your husband can't ever seem to get his dirty shirts into a hamper. So there are hard changes and easy changes.

What distinguishes one from the other? In this chapter , we argue that successful changes share a common pattern. They require the leader of the change to do three things at once. We've already mentioned one of those three things

To change someone's behavior, you've got to change that person's situation. ,   The situation isn't the whole game, of course. You can send an alcoholic to rehab, where the new environment will help him go dry. But what happens when he leaves and loses that influence? You might see a boost in productivity from your sales reps when the sales manager shadows them, but what happens afterward when the situation returns to normal? For individuals' behavior to change, you've got to influence not only their environment but their hearts and minds.

The problem is this: Oftentimes   the heart and mind disagree Fervently Considering   the Clocky, an alarm clock invented by an MIT student, Gauri Nanda. It's no ordinary alarm clock-it has wheels. You set it at night, and in the morning when the alarm goes off, it rolls off your nightstand and scurries around the room, forcing you to chase it down. Picture the scene. You're crawling around the bedroom in your underwear, stalking and cursing a runaway clock. Clocky ensures that you won't snooze-button your way to disaster. And apparently that's a common fear, since about 35,000 units were purchased, at $50 each, in Clocky's first two years on the market (despite minimal marketing). The success of this invention reveals a lot about human psychology. What it shows, fundamentally, is that we are schizophrenic. Part of us-our rational side-wants to get up at 5:45 a.m., allowing ourselves plenty of time for a quick jog before we leave for the office. The other part of us-the emotional side-wakes up in the darkness of the early morning, snoozing inside a warm cocoon of sheets and blankets, and wants nothing in the world so much as a few more minutes of sleep.

If, like us, your   Three Surprises About Change emotional side tends to win these internal debates, then you might be a potential Clocky customer. The beauty of the device is that it allows your rational side to outsmart your emotional side. It's simply impossible to stay cuddled up under the covers when a rogue alarm clock is rolling around your room. Let's be blunt here: Clocky is not a product for a sane species. If Spock wants to get up at 5:45 a.m., he'll just get up. No drama required. Our built-in schizophrenia is a deeply weird thing, but we don't think much about it because we're so used to it. When we kick off a new diet, we toss the Cheetos and Oreos out of the pantry, because our rational side knows that when our emotional side gets a craving, there's no hope of self-control.

The only option is to remove the temptation altogether. (For the record, some MIT student will make a fortune designing Cheetos that scurry away from people when they're on a diet.) The unavoidable conclusion is this: Your brain isn't of one mind. The conventional wisdom in psychology, in fact, is that the brain has two independent systems at work at all times. First, there's what we called the emotional side. It's the part of you that is instinctive, that feels pain and pleasure.

Second, there's the rational side, also known as the reflective or conscious system. It's the part of you that deliberates and analyzes and looks into the future. In the past few decades, psychologists have learned a lot about these two systems, but of course mankind has always been aware of the tension. Plato said that in our heads we have a rational charioteer who has to rein in an unruly horse that "barely yields to horsewhip and goad combined." Freud wrote about the selfish id and the conscientious superego (and also about the ego, which the three surprises changes plan, to think beyond the moment (all those things that your pet can't do). .

Drawing a point of change with the animal called elephant

But what may surprise you is that the Elephant also has enormous strengths and that the Rider has crippling weaknesses. The Elephant isn't always the bad guy. Emotion is the Elephant's turf-love and compassion and sympathy and loyalty. That fierce instinct you have to protect your kids against harm-that's the Elephant. That spine-stiffening you feel when you need to stand up for yourself-that's the Elephant. And even more important if you're contemplating a change, the   Elephant is the one who gets things done. To make progress toward a goal, whether it's noble or crass, requires the energy and drive of the Elephant. And this strength is the mirror image of the Rider's great weakness: spinning his wheels. The Rider tends to over-analyze and over-think things. Chances are, you know people with Rider problems: your friend who can agonize for twenty minutes about what to eat for dinner; your colleague who can brainstorm about new ideas for hours but can't ever seem to make a decision. If you want to change things, you've got to appeal to both. The Rider provides the planning and direction, and the Elephant provides the energy. So if you reach the Riders of your team but not the Elephants, team members will have understanding without motivation. If you reach their Elephants but not their Riders, they'll have passion without direction. In both cases, the flaws can be paralyzing. A reluctant Elephant and a wheel-spinning Rider can both ensure that nothing changes. But when Elephants and Riders move together, change can come easily.

When Rider and Elephant disagree about which way to move, you've got a problem. The Rider can get his way temporarily in which the three

     THE POWER OF POSITIVE MIND

changes   can tug on the reins hard enough to get the Elephant to submit. (Anytime you use willpower you're doing exactly that.)

But the Rider can't win a tug-of-war with a huge animal for long. He simply gets exhausted. To see this point more clearly, consider the behavior of some college students who participated in a study about "food perception" (or so they were told). They reported to the lab a bit hungry; they'd been asked not to eat for at least three hours beforehand. They were led to a room that smelled amazing the researchers had just baked chocolate-chip cookies. On a table in the center of the room were two bowls. One held a sampling of chocolates, along with the warm, fresh-baked chocolate-chip cookies they'd smelled. The other bowl held a bunch of radishes. The researchers had prepped a cover story: We've selected chocolates and radishes because they have highly distinctive tastes. Tomorrow, we'll contact you and ask about your memory of the taste sensations you experienced while eating them. Half the participants were asked to eat two or three cookies and some chocolate candies, but no radishes.

The other half were asked to eat at least two or three radishes, but no cookies. While they ate, the researchers left the room, intending, rather sadistically, to induce temptation: They wanted those poor radish-eaters to sit there, alone, nibbling on rabbit food, glancing enviously at the fresh-baked cookies. (It probably goes without saying that the cookie-eaters experienced no great struggle in resisting the radishes.)

 Despite the temptation, all participants ate what they were asked to eat, and none of the radish-eaters snuck a cookie. That's willpower at work. At that point, the "taste study" was officially over, and another group of researchers entered with a second, supposedly unrelated study: We're trying to find who's better at solving problems,

The three change surprised the   college students or high school students. This framing was intended to get the college students to puff out their chests and take the forthcoming task seriously.

The college students were presented with a series of puzzles that required them to trace a complicated geometric shape without retracing any lines

        THE POWER OF POSITIVE MIND

and without lifting their pencils from the paper. They were given multiple sheets of paper so they could try over and over. In reality, the puzzles were designed to be unsolvable.

 The researchers wanted to see how long the college students would persist in a difficult, frustrating task before they finally gave up. The "untempted" students, who had not had to resist eating the chocolate-chip cookies, spent nineteen minutes on the task, making thirty-four well-intentioned attempts to solve the problem. The radish-eaters were less persistent. They gave up after only eight minutes-less that:I half the time spent by the cookie eaters-and they managed only nineteen solution attempts. Why did they quit so easily? The answer may surprise you: They ran out of self·control. In studies like this one, psychologists have discovered .that self-control is an exhaustible resource. It's like doing bench presses at the gym. The first one is easy, when your muscles are fresh. But with each additional repetition, your muscles get more exhausted, until you can't lift the bar again. The radish-eaters had drained their self-control by resisting the cookies. So when their Elephants, inevitably, started complaining about the puzzle task-its too hard, it's no fun, we're no good at this-their Riders didn't have enough strength to yank on the reins for more than eight minutes. Meanwhile, the cookie-eaters had a fresh, untaxed Rider, who fought off the Elephant for nineteen minutes. Self-control is an exhaustible resource. This is a crucial realization, because when we talk about "self-control," we don't mean just the   Changes we encounter   as in the willpower needed to fight vices (smokes, cookies, alcohol).

We're talking about a broader kind of self-supervision. Think of the way your mind works when you're giving negative feedback to an employee, or assembling a new bookshelf, or learning a new dance. You are careful and deliberate with your words or movements. It feels like there's a supervisor on duty. That's self-control, too. Contrast that with all the situations in which your behavior doesn't feel "supervised"-for instance, the sensation while you're driving that you can't remember the last few miles of road, or the easy, unthinking way you take a shower or make your morning coffee. Much of our daily behavior, in fact, is more

   THE POWER OF POSITIVE MIND

automatic than supervised, and that's a good thing because the supervised behavior is the hard stuff. It's draining.

Dozens of studies have demonstrated the exhausting nature of self-supervision. For instance, people who were asked to make tricky choices and trade-offs-such as setting up a wedding registry or ordering a new computer-were worse at focusing and solving problems than others who hadn't made the tough choices. In one study, some people were asked to restrain their emotions while watching a sad movie about sick animals. Afterward, they exhibited less physical endurance than others who'd let the tears flow freely.

The research shows that we burn up self-control in a wide variety of situations: managing the impression we're making on others; coping with fears; controlling our spending; trying to focus on simple instructions such as "Don't think of a white bear"; and many, many others. Here's why this matters for change: When people try to change things, they're usually tinkering with behaviors that have become automatic, and changing those behaviors requires careful supervision by the Rider. The bigger the change you're suggesting, the more it will sap people's self-control.

Three surprises About Change And when people exhaust their self-control, what they're exhausting are the mental muscles needed to think creatively, to focus, to inhibit their impulses, and to persist in the face of frustration or failure. In other words, they're exhausting precisely the mental muscles needed to make a big change. So when you hear people say that change is hard because people are lazy or resistant, that's just Rat wrong.

In fact, the opposite is true: Change is hard because people wear themselves out. And that's the second surprise about change: What looks like laziness is often exhaustion.   Jon Stegner believed the company he worked for, a large manufacturer, was wasting vast sums of money. "I thought we had an opportunity to drive down purchasing costs not by 2 percent but by something on the order of $1 billion over the next five years," said Stegner, who is quoted in John Kotter and Dan Cohen's essential book The Heart of Change. To reap these savings, a big process shift would be required, and for that shift to occur, Stegner knew that he'd have to convince his bosses.

He also knew that they'd never embrace such a big shift unless they believed in the opportunity, and for the most part, they didn't. Seeking a compelling example of the company's poor purchasing habits, Stegner assigned a summer student intern to investigate a single item-work gloves, which workers in most of the company's factories wore. The student embarked on a mission to identify all the types of gloves used in all the company's factories and then trace back what the company was paying for them. The intrepid intern soon reported that the factories were Three Surprises About Change   purchasing 424 different kinds of gloves! Furthermore, they were using different glove suppliers, and they were all negotiating their own prices.

The same pair of gloves that cost $5 at one factory might cost $17 at another. At Stegner's request, the student collected a specimen of every one of the 424 different types of gloves and tagged each with the price paid.

Then all the gloves were gathered up, brought to the boardroom, and piled up on the conference table. Stegner invited all the division presidents to come visit the Glove Shrine. He recalled the scene: What they saw was a large expensive table, normally clean or with a few papers, now stacked high with gloves. Each of our executives stared at this display for a minute. Then each said something like, "We really buy all these different kinds of gloves?" Well, as a matter of fact, yes we do. "Really?" Yes, really. Then they walked around the table .. .. They could see the prices. They looked at two gloves that seemed exactly alike, yet one was marked $3.22 and the other $10.55. It's a rare event when these people don't have anything to say. But that day, they just stood with their mouths gaping. The gloves exhibit soon became a traveling road show, visiting dozens of plants.

The reaction was visceral: This is crazy. We're crazy. And we've got to make sure this stops happening. Soon Stegner had exactly the mandate for change that he'd sought. The company changed its purchasing process and saved a great deal of money. This was exactly the happy ending everyone wanted (except, of course, for the glove salesmen who'd managed to sell the $5 gloves for $17).

Let's be honest: Most of us would not have tried what Stegner did. It would have been so easy, so natural, to make a presentation that spoke only to the Rider. Think of the possibilities: the spreadsheets, the savings data, the cost-cutting protocols, the recommendations for supplier consolidation, the exquisite logic for central purchasing. You could have created a 12-tabbed Microsoft Excel spreadsheet that would have made a tax accountant weep with joy. But instead of doing any of that, Stegner dumped a bunch of gloves on a table and invited his bosses to see them. If there is such a thing as white-collar courage, surely this was an instance. Stegner knew that if things were going to change, he had to get his colleagues' Elephants on his side. If he had made an analytical appeal, he probably would have gotten some supportive nods, and the execs might have requested a follow-up meeting six weeks later (and then rescheduled it).

The analytical case was compelling-by itself, it might have convinced Stegner's colleagues that overhauling the purchasing system would be an important thing to do ... next year. Remember that if you reach your colleagues' Riders but not their Elephants, they will have direction without motivation. Maybe their Riders will drag the Elephant down the road for a while, but as we've seen, that effort can't last long. Once you break through to feeling, though, things change.

Stegner delivered a jolt to his colleagues. First, they thought to themselves, were crazy! Then they thought, we can fix this. Everyone could think of a few things to try to fix the glove problem and by extension the ordering process as a whole. That got their Elephants fired up to move. We don't expect potential billion-dollar change stories to come dressed up like this. The change effort was led by a single employee, Three Surprises About Change 15 with the able help of a summer intern. It focused on a single product. The scope of the presentation didn't correspond in any way to the scope of the proposal.

Yet Stegner's strategy worked. That's the power of speaking to both the Rider and the Elephant and that could only have being   possible due to power of change in the mind . in summary , 'NOTHING AFFECTS YOUR CHOICES IN LIFE AND MANIFESTS PHYSICALLY UNTIL THERE IS A   MENTAL SHIFT AND RE-ORIENTATION FROM THE NORMAL '

Chapter

Six

REVIEW YOUR ROUTINE

One Saturday in 2000, some unsuspecting moviegoers showed up at a suburban theater in Chicago to catch a 1 :05 p.m. matinee of Mel Gibson's action flick Payback. They were handed a soft drink and a free bucket of popcorn and were asked to stick around after the movie to answer a few questions about the concession stand. These movie fans were unwitting participants in a study of irrational eating behavior. There was something unusual about the popcorn they received. It was wretched. In fact, it had been carefully engineered to be wretched. It had been popped five days earlier and was so stale that it squeaked when you ate it. One moviegoer later compared it to Styrofoam packing peanuts, and two others, forgetting that they'd received the popcorn for free, demanded their money back. Some of them got their free popcorn in a medium-size bucket, 2 T hree S u r p rises A b out Change and others got a large bucket-the sort of huge tub that looks like it might once have been an above-ground swimming pool. Every person got a bucket so there'd be no need to share. The researchers responsible for the study were interested in a simple question: Would the people with bigger buckets eat more?

Both buckets were so big that none of the moviegoers could finish their individual portions. So the actual research question was a bit more specific: Would somebody with a larger inexhaustible supply of popcorn eat more than someone with a smaller inexhaustible supply? The sneaky researchers weighed the buckets before and after the movie, so they were able to measure precisely how much popcorn each person ate. The results were stunning: People with the large buckets ate 53 percent more popcorn than people with the medium size. That's the equivalent of 173 more calories and approximately 21 extra hand-dips into the bucket. Brian Wansink, the author of the study, runs the Food and Brand Lab at Cornell University, and he described the results in his book Mindless Eating: "We've run other popcorn studies, and the results were always the same, however we tweaked the details. It didn't matter if our moviegoers were in Pennsylvania, Illinois, or Iowa, and it didn't matter what kind of movie was showing; all of our popcorn studies led to the same conclusion. People eat more when you give them a bigger container. Period." No other theory explains the behavior. These people weren't eating for pleasure. (The popcorn was so stale it squeaked!) They weren't driven by a desire to finish their portion. (Both buckets were too big to finish.) It didn't matter whether they were hungry or full.

The equation is unyielding: Bigger container = more eating. Best of all, people refused to believe the results. After the movie, the researchers told the moviegoers about the two bucket sizes and the findings of their past research. The researchers asked, Do you think you ate more because of the larger size? The majority scoffed at the idea, saying, "Things like that don't trick me," or, "I'm pretty good at knowing when I'm full."

. Imagine that someone showed you the data from the   popcorn eating study but didn't mention the bucket sizes. On your data summary, you could quickly scan the results and see how much popcorn different people ate-some people ate a little, some ate a lot, and some seemed to be testing the physical limits of the human stomach. Armed with a data set like that, you would find it easy to jump to conclusions. Some people are Reasonable Snackers, and others are Big Gluttons. A public-health expert, studying that data alongside you, would likely get very worried about the Gluttons.

We need to motivate these people to adopt healthier snacking behaviors! Let's find ways to show them the health hazards of eating so much! But wait a second. If you want people to eat less popcorn, the solutionis pretty simple: Give them smaller buckets. You don't have to worry about their knowledge or their attitudes. You can see how easy it would be to turn an easy change problem (shrinking people's buckets) into a hard change problem (convincing people to think differently).

And that's the first surprise about change: What looks like a people problem is often a situation problem. This is a chapter to help you change things. We consider change at every level-individual, organizational, and societal. Three Surprises About Change want to help your brother beat his gambling addiction. Maybe you need your team at work to act more frugally because of market conditions. Maybe you wish more of your neighbors would bike to work. Usually these topics are treated separately-there is "change management" advice for executives and "self-help" advice for individuals and "change the world" advice for activists. That's a shame, because all change efforts have something in common: For anything to change, someone has to start acting differently. Your brother has got to stay out of the casino; your employees have got to start booking coach fares. Ultimately, all change efforts boil down to the same mission: Can you get people to start behaving in a new way?We know what you're thinking-people resist change. But it's not quite that easy. Babies are born every day to parents who, inexplicably, welcome the change. Think about the sheer magnitude of that change!Would anyone agree to work for a boss who'd wake you up twice a night, screaming, for trivial administrative duties? (And what if, everytime you wore a new piece of clothing, the boss spit up on it?) Yet people don't resist this massive change-they volunteer for it. In our lives, we embrace lots of big changes-not only babies, but marriages and new homes and new technologies and new job duties. Meanwhile,other behaviors are maddeningly intractable. Smokers keep smoking and kids grow fatter and your husband can't ever seem to get his dirty shirts into a hamper. So there are hard changes and easy changes.

What distinguishes one from the other? In this book, we argue that successful changes share a common pattern. They require the leader of the change to do three things at once. We've already mentioned oneof those three things: To change someone's behavior, you've got to change that person's situation.   The situation isn't the whole game, of course. You can send an alcoholic torehab, where the new environment will help him go dry. But what happens when he leaves and loses that influence? You might see a boost in productivity from your sales reps when the sales manager shadows them, but what happens afterward when the situation returns to normal? For individuals' behavior to change, you've got to influence not only their environment but their hearts and minds. The problem is this: Often the heart and mind disagree.

Consider the Clocky, an alarm clock invented by an MIT student, Gauri Nanda. It's no ordinary alarm clock-it has wheels. You set it at night, and in the morning when the alarm goes off, it rolls off your nightstand and scurries around the room, forcing you to chase it down. Picture the scene: You're crawling around the bedroom in your underwear, stalking and cursing a runaway clock. Clocky ensures that you won't snooze-button your way to disaster. And apparently that's a common fear, since about 35,000 units were purchased, at $50 each, in Clocky's first two years on the market (despite minimal marketing). The success of this invention reveals a lot about human psychology.

What it shows, fundamentally, is that we are schizophrenic. Part of us-our rational side-wants to get up at 5:45 a.m., allowing ourselves

plenty of time for a quick jog before we leave for the office. The other part of us-the emotional sidewakes up in the darkness of the early morning, snoozing inside a warm cocoon of sheets and blankets, and wants nothing in the world so much as a few more minutes of sleep.

If, like us, your 6 Three Surpri ses About Change emotional side tends to win these internal debates, then you might be a potential Clocky customer. The beauty of the device is that it allows your rational side to outsmart your emotional side. It's simply impossible tostay cuddled up under the covers when a rogue alarm clock is rolling around your room. Let's be blunt here: Clocky is not a product for a sane species. If Spock wants to get up at 5:45 a.m., he'll just get up.

No drama required. Our built-in schizophrenia is a deeply weird thing, but we don't think much about it because we're so used to it. When we kick off a new diet, we toss the Cheetos and Oreos out of the pantry, because our rational side knows that when our emotional side gets a craving, there's no hope of self-control. The only option is to remove the temptation altogether. (For the record, some MIT student will make a fortune designing Cheetos that scurry away from people when they're on a diet.) The unavoidable conclusion is this: Your brain isn't of one mind. The conventional wisdom in psychology, in fact, is that the brain has two independent systems at work at all times. First, there's what we called the emotional side. It's the part of you that is instinctive, that feels pain and pleasure. Second,there's the rational side, also known as the reflective or conscious system. It's the part of you that deliberates and analyzes and looks intothe future. In the past few decades, psychologists have learned a lot about these two systems, but of course mankind has always been aware of the tension. Plato said that in our heads we have a rational charioteer who has to rein in an unruly horse that "barely yields to horsewhip and goad combined." Freud wrote about the selfish id and the conscientious superego (and also about the ego,, to think beyond the moment (all those things that your pet can't do). But what may surprise you is that the Elephant also has enormous strengths and that the Rider has crippling weaknesses. The Elephant isn't always the bad guy. Emotion is the Elephant's turf-love and compassion and sympathy and loyalty. That fierce instinct you have to protect your kids against harm-that's the Elephant. That spine-stiffening you feel when you need to stand up for yourself-that's the Elephant. And even more important if you're contemplating a change, the . Elephant is the one who gets things done. To make progress toward a goal, whether it's noble or crass, requires the energy and drive of the Elephant. And this strength is the mirror image of the Rider's great weakness: spinning his wheels. The Rider tends to over analyze and over think things. Chances are, you know people with Rider problems: your friend who can agonize for twenty minutes about what to eat for dinner.

. If you want to change things, you've got to appeal to both. The Rider provides the planning and direction, and the Elephant provides the energy. So if you reach the Riders of your team but notthe Elephants, team members will have understanding without motivation. If you reach their Elephants but not their Riders, they'll have passion without direction. In both cases, the flaws can be paralyzing. A reluctant Elephant and a wheel-spinning Rider can bothensure that nothing changes. But when Elephants and Riders move together, change can come easily. When Rider and Elephant disagree about which way to move, you've got a problem. The Rider can get his way temporarily-the Three Surprises About Change   can tug on the reins hard enough to get the Elephant to submit. (Anytime you use willpower you're doing exactly that.) But the Rider can't win a tug-of-war with a huge animal for long. He simply gets exhausted. To see this point more clearly, consider the behavior of some college students who participated in a study about "food perception" (or so they were told). They reported to the lab a bit hungry; they'd been asked not to eat for at least three hours beforehand. They were led to a room that smelled amazing the researchers had just baked chocolate-chip cookies. On a table in the center of the room were two bowls. One held a sampling of chocolates, along with the warm, fresh-baked chocolate-chip cookies they'd smelled. The other bowl held a bunch of radishes. The researchers had prepped a cover story: We've selected chocolates and radishes because they have highly distinctive tastes. Tomorrow, we'll contact you and ask about your memory of the taste sensations you experienced while eating them. Half the participants were asked to eattwo or three cookies and some chocolate candies, but no radishes. Theother half were asked to eat at least two or three radishes, but no cookies. While they ate, the researchers left the room, intending, rather sadistically, to induce temptation: They wanted those poor radish-eaters to sit there, alone, nibbling on rabbit food, glancing enviously at the fresh-baked cookies. (It probably goes without sayingthat the cookie-eaters experienced no great struggle in resisting the radishes.) Despite the temptation, all participants ate what they were asked to eat, and none of the radish-eaters snuck a cookie. That's willpower at work. At that point, the "taste study" was officially over, and another group of researchers entered with a second, supposedly unrelated study: We're trying to find who's better at solving problems, Three Surprises About Change college students or high school students. This framing was intended to get the college students to puff out their chests and take the forthcoming task seriously. The college students were presented with a series of puzzles that required them to trace a complicated geometric shape without retracing any lines and without lifting their pencils from the paper. They were given multiple sheets of paper so they could try over and over. In reality, the puzzles were designed to be unsolvable. The researchers wanted to see how long the college students would persist in a difficult, frustrating task before they finally gave up. The "untempted" students, who had not had to resist eating the chocolate-chip cookies, spent nineteen minutes on the task, making thirty-four well-intentioned attempts to solve the problem. The radish-eaters were less persistent. They gave up after only eight minutes-less that:I half the time spent by the   - and they managed only nineteen solution attempts. Why did they quit so easily? The answer may surprise you: They ran out of self·control. In studies like this one, psychologists have discovered .that self-controlis an exhaustible resource. It's like doing bench presses at the gym.

The first one is easy, when your muscles are fresh. But with each additional repetition, your muscles get more exhausted, until you can't lift the bar again. The radish-eaters had drained their self-control by resisting the cookies. So when their Elephants, inevitably, started complaining about the puzzle task-its too hard, it's no fun, we're no good at this-their Riders didn't have enough strength to yank on the reins for more than eight minutes. Meanwhile, the cookie-eaters had a fresh, untaxed Rider, who fought off the Elephant for nineteen minutes. Self-control is an exhaustible resource. This is a crucial realization, because when we talk about "self-control," we don't mean Three Surprises About Change.

The narrow sense of the word, asin the willpower needed to fight vice (smokes, cookies, alcohol).

We're talking about a broader kind of self-supervision. Think of the way your mind works when you're giving negative feedback to an employee, or assembling a new bookshelf, or learning a new dance. You are careful and deliberate with your words or movements. It feels like there's a supervisor on duty.

That's self-control, too. Contrast thatwith all the situations in which your behavior doesn't feel "supervised"-for instance, the sensation while you're driving that you can't remember the last few miles of road, or the easy, unthinking wayyou take a shower or make your morning coffee. Much of our daily behavior, in fact, is more automatic than supervised, and that's a goodthing because the supervised behavior is the hard stuff.

It's draining dozens of studies have demonstrated the exhausting nature of self- supervision. For instance, people who were asked to make tricky choices and trade-offs-such as setting up a wedding registry or ordering a new computer-were worse at focusing and solving problems than others who hadn't made the tough choices. In one study, some people were asked to restrain their emotions while watching a sad movie about sick animals. Afterward, they exhibitedless physical endurance than others who'd let the tears flow freely.

The research shows that we burn up self-control in a wide variety of situations: managing the impression we're making on others; coping with fears; controlling our spending; trying to focus on simple instructions such as "Don't think of a white bear"; and many, many others. Here's why this matters for change: When people try to change things, they're usually tinkering with behaviors that have become automatic, and changing those behaviors requires careful supervision by the Rider. The bigger the change you're suggesting, the more it will sap people's self-control.   Another part of changes is   when people exhaust their self-control, which are their   mental muscles needed to think creatively, to focus, to inhibit their impulses, and to persist in the face of frustration or failure. In other words, they're exhausting precisely the mental muscles needed to make a big change. So when you hear people say that change is hard because people are lazy or

          THE POWER OF POSITIVE MIND

resistant, that's j ust Rat wrong. In fact, the opposite is true: Change is hard because people wear themselves out. And that's the second surprise about change: What looks like laziness is often exhaustion.   Jon Stegner believed the company he worked for, a large manufacturer, was wasting vast sums of money. "I thought we had an opportunity to drive down purchasing costs not by two percent but by something on the order of $1 billion over the next five years," said Stegner, who is quoted in John Kotter and Dan Cohen's essential book The Heart of Change. To reap these savings, a big process shift would be required, and for that shift to occur, Stegner knew that he'd have to convince his bosses. He also knew that they'd never embrace such a big shift unless they believed in the opportunity, and for the most part, they didn't. Seeking a compelling example of the company's poor purchasing habits, Stegner assigned a summer student intern to investigate a single item-work gloves, which workers in most of the company's factories wore. The student embarked on a mission to identify all the types of gloves used in all the company's factories and then trace back what the company was paying for them. The intrepid intern soon reported that the factories were Three Surprises About Change purchasing 424 different kinds of gloves! Furthermore, they were using different glove suppliers, and they were all negotiating their own prices. The same pair of gloves that cost $5 at one factory might cost $17 at another. At Stegner's request, the student collected a specimen of every one of the 424 different types of gloves and tagged each with the price paid. Then all the gloves were gathered up, brought to the boardroom, and piled up on the conference table.

Stegner invited all the division presidents to come visit the Glove Shrine. He recalled thescene: What they saw was a large expensive table, normally clean or with a few papers, now stacked high with gloves. Each of our executives stared at this display for a minute. Then each said something like, "We really buy all these different kinds of gloves?" Well, as a matter of fact, yes we do. "Really?" Yes, really. Then they walked around the table .. .. They could see the prices. They looked attwo gloves that seemed exactly alike, yet one was marked $3.22 and the other $10.55. It's a rare event when these people don't have anything to say. But that day, they just stood with their mouth gaping .

     THE POWER OF POSITIVE MIND

The gloves exhibit soon became a traveling road show, visiting dozens of plants. The reaction was visceral: This is crazy. We're crazy. And we've got to make sure this stops happening. Soon Stegner had exactly the mandate for change that he'd sought. The company changed its purchasing process and saved a great deal of money. This was exactly the happy ending everyone wanted (except, of course, for the glove salesmen who'd managed to sell the $5 glovesfor $17).

 Let's be honest: Most of us would not have tried what Stegner did. It would have been so easy, so natural, to make a presentation that spoke only to the Rider. Think of the possibilities: the spreadsheets, the savings data, the cost-cutting protocols, the recommendations for supplier consolidation, the exquisite logic for central purchasing. You could have created a 12-tabbed Microsoft Excel spreadsheet that would have made a tax accountant weep with joy. But instead of doing any of that, Stegner dumped a bunch of gloves on a table and invited his bosses to see them. If there is such a thing as white-collar courage, surely this was an instance.

Stegner knew that if things were going to change, he had to get his colleagues' Elephants on his side. If he had made an analytical appeal, he probably would have gotten some supportive nods, and the execs might have requested a follow-up meeting six weeks later (and then rescheduled it). The analytical case was compelling-by itself, it might have convinced Stegner's colleagues that overhauling the purchasing system would be an important thing to do ... next year. Remember that if you reach your colleagues' Riders but not their Elephants, they will have direction without motivation. Maybe their Riders will drag the Elephant down the road for a while, but as we've seen, that effort can't last long. Onceyou break through to feeling, though, things change. Stegner delivered a jolt to his colleagues. First, they thought to themselves, were crazy! Then they thought, we can fix this. Everyone could think of a few things to try to fix the glove problem and by extension the ordering process as a whole. That got their Elephants fired up to move. We don't expect potential billion-dollar change stories to come dressed up like this. The change effort was led by a single employee.

It's Great to Change Your Mind About What You Want to Do

The society doesn't normally support this notion — but it's perfectly fine to change your mind. In fact, it's often a clear sign that you're growing and progressing on your goals.

If you never change your mind about anything, it may mean that you're not alive. Or that you just aren't willing to learn anymore.

I used to believe that frequently changing my mind about what I wanted to do meant that there was something wrong with me. Friends and family would reprimand me: *"you can't be constantly changing your mind!"* Or offering advice: *"just pick something — anything — and stick to it."*

There was a time I believed their words and I thought I needed to fix myself to live my life successfully.

The good news is that you don't need to believe this. Because what would you rather do: stick with doing something you don't enjoy for the rest of your life — or change your mind?

You Don't Have to Embrace Other People's Beliefs as Your Own
Chances are you've been told that changing your mind frequently isn't beneficial.

It leads to unfinished projects, destroyed trust and wasted resources. It's also a sign that you don't know what you want in life, you're inconsistent and you can't bear the consequences of our deeds.

Not exactly the greatest predictors for your future. Or so they tell you.

I used to be one of these inconsistent, irresponsible and indeterminate people. I would engage in a project just to move on to another one in due time.

At the end of college, I became invested in academic research and spent a lot of my time on that. Then I found a travel agency I wanted to work for. But after a few months, my friends and I came up with anidea for an art project — so I decided to leave the travel agency and throw myself into the world of immersive theatre.

After we staged our first plays, I realized this wasn't the kind of workI wanted to do either.

Despite feeling guilty towards my friends, I left the project. I needed more time for myself. At the time, I was discovering the world of spiritual growth and emotional processing and I realized that those discoveries were calling for my attention.

After a good deal of working with my feelings — I started writing again. I moved homes and countries a few times. I worked in different jobs and made friends with people from various backgrounds.

Those who knew me at that time would say without hesitation that I was *constantly* changing my mind. Some even referred to me as a "lost soul."

But this wasn't how I would describe myself. I was just curious to verify what I did and didn't like doing. I enjoyed learning new skills and discovering things about myself I hadn't been aware of.

Changing my mind about what I wanted to do was just a natural consequence of those discoveries. And it wasn't a problem as far as I was concerned.

Problems arose only when I took other people's opinions as more important than my own. Some of those people openly disapproved of what I was doing. In essence, they were just expressing that they wouldn't want to live their lives the way I did. Fair enough.

But I took it personally. I felt like I had to defend my way of living by confronting other people's judgments. This sometimes caused me to trust their opinions about my life more than I trusted myself.

Even though I knew I was doing my best to lay the foundation for more serious decisions in the future — I still listened to the naysayers. It felt scary when they said things like: *"If you keep changing your mind all the time, you will waste your life."*

What if they were right and I was indeed setting myself up for something terrible, despite my best intentions?

Luckily, even when I felt afraid, I somehow managed to nurture an alternative belief about my life. A belief that was more in tune with me.

In this new paradigm, the fact that I changed my mind so often meant something different.

It was an indicator of me being flexible, open-minded and curious — rather than careless or unreliable. It was a sign that I was evolving and learning — and so, my mind and ideas about what I wanted were changing, too.

At some point, I observed that jumping between various environments, jobs and friends was actually helping me to pinpoint what remained *unchanged.*

Why Changing Your Mind Is Necessary

In Polish, there is a proverb saying that "only cows don't change their minds." That is to say that humans do — and should.

Especially humans who are in love with life and want to make the most of it.

I realize now that what other people called *changing my mind* was just an external expression of my internal process. This process was all about **figuring out the best way to live my life by following my curiosity.**

Changing your mind isn't a sign that there's something wrong with you or that you're setting yourself up for failure. It's just a social habit to interpret it this way. In reality, changing your mind is simplya reflection of all the internal changes going on inside of you.

It's more of an effect than a cause.

"I wondered why changing one's mind is often so difficult. After all, both the world and our view of it are constantly changing; circumstances never remain static, so why should our responses to them be forever locked in their initial form?" — Alex Lickerman, Changing Your Mind

The truth is that everyone has to change their mind once in a while. Otherwise, you'd be now stuck with the decisions you made when you were five! A lot has changed in your life since then — so your decisions and ideas naturally change, too.

From this perspective, the pace at which you're changing your mind can be seen as a function of the pace at which you're growing. The more new data you collect through your experience, the more complex the picture of your life becomes.

As this happens, the vision for your future naturally adjusts. Some people call it "changing your mind."

But you can call this process differently. Now that we dug into what "changing your mind" actually is, we can look for a more suitable language to describe it.

<u>"Changing Your Mind" versus "Adjusting Your Vision"The words we use to describe our lives matter.</u> **Language conditions the way we interpret our experiences.**

<u>Therefore, the phrase I prefer </u>to use instead of "changing your mind"is "adjusting your vision." It alters the way we perceive ourselves andour choices in the context of creating the life we want.

- **Changing your mind** indicates that you feel lost, undecided and that you rely mainly on the external factors to navigate your life.
- **Adjusting your vision** suggests that there is a consistent intention behind all your deeds. It doesn't matter if you don't realize it consciously yet — the intention is always there. The process of *adjusting your vision* is a part of uncovering this intention.

But how does adjusting your vision play out in real life?

As I jumped between different environments and jobs, I realized that no matter what the context was, I always looked for opportunities to **write something.**

I was — at first, unconsciously — using all of my seemingly random experiences as my writing playground. Each of them served a purposein establishing my confidence as a writer.

I didn't realize this in the beginning. At first, all the different jobs and circumstances appeared as just "me trying new things". But because I observed myself through these experiences, I started noticing a persisting truth.

I wanted to write wherever I was. I just lacked confidence that this could be something more than an indulgent hobby. So I travelled and tested myself in different circumstances to accumulate this confidence.

I was building my momentum by reconfirming, over and over again,that writing is one of the few constants in my life — no matter what.

Finally, the time came to get rid of the distractions and make a firm decision. I established enough trust in my consistency and willingnessas a writer. I simply saw writing as my best shot at building a successful and rewarding career.

By adjusting my vision through many iterations, I got to the point where I didn't see anything I would pursue more happily.

Paradoxically, what appeared to be "changing my mind" in the beginning, led me to the firmest and most informed decision of my life.

I decided to become a full-time writer. Regardless of how much I would still need to adjust my vision in the process.

Adjusting Vision Is Inevitable in Pursuing Your Dreams

Because you're still reading this article, I assume that going after your dreams is important to you. You may even already have an idea of how to do that.

But do I sense that there's still something holding you back?

For most of us, this something is fear. Not just the fear of failure and not being good enough. It's also the fear of having to change your plans. The fear that it may be necessary to adjust your vision and let go of control sometimes.

This fear is natural, but also possible to surpass. In essence, all it takesis one decision — to ***just do it***.

Once you've tested the waters for long enough, you start trusting in your ability to swim. And if you can swim, you're ready to go offshore and leave the future open, trusting that you'll be able to get across the lake.

Even if a current takes you off course — that's fine. You can't prepare for it in advance, but you know you're a strong enough swimmer to adjust to the situation. There's always a way to adjust.

In fact, there are countless ways. Sometimes it will be fighting against the waves and sometimes — letting the water carry you when the wind blows too hard. But you will only be able to see what you need to do *after you've left the shore*.

Once you take the leap, keep in mind that the adjustments to your course are only that — adjustments. They don't mean you're abandoning your original idea. They don't mean you're screwing up.

All you're doing is refining your vision as you gain more information, experience and clarity on your goals. Adjusting your vision is a sign that you're actively pursuing it. That you're learning from your mistakes. That you're being open and flexible.

You can call it as you like. On the surface, it may seem like you're "changing your mind" all the time. But as long as you know what you're truly committed to — or you're actively trying to discover it

— these changes are beneficial.

So don't be afraid to change. Leave the shore, swim as best as you can, and prepare yourself to adjust the course.

Chapter **Seven**

STIR UP THE GIFT IN AND WITHIN YOU.

Is everybody on earth gifted? Does everyone have talents or are there "gift-less" people somewhere on the surface of the earth? Are some people more endowed than others? …and are there some that aren't endowed at all? Now here's the big one …Are you gifted or gift-less? These questions bug the minds of many people all across the earth as they try to discover themselves and come to a point of self realization. Many have grown frustrated with their lives and are full of nativities in their minds. If you are striving hard to have a fulfilled life and you've answered those questions correctly, then you are one step closer to making the most of your time on earth. Whether or not you were able to answer my questions however, you'll definitely find my summations that will follow from this point thought-provoking. Everyone on earth has potentials! There are no empty men on earth, but there are many people with wrong perceptions of who they are and what they carry. Also, there are no "gift-less" people on earth, but there are many people who don't even know how gifted they are. Nothing devalues a man than having a sense of emptiness and incapacity. It is the understanding of who you are that determines what you become. How you see yourself consistently determines what you become perpetually. It is often said that "in every man, there is a seed of greatness." When this seed is nurtured, it can catapult him from where he is to where God wants him to be. Every bird in the sky is gifted to fly. Every fish in the ocean is gifted to swim. Similarly, everyone on earth is gifted to do something special. Click here or copy to make a donation to this author:

No purpose is ever accomplished without a discovered, developed and functional talent. You may have big dreams, but if you don't identify the talents that will make those dreams a reality and develop them, the dreams may end a mirage. A talent is simply a 'Gift' from God to a man. It is often referred to as "gifting"; that special endowment within you. It is unique to you and can turn you from a mediocre into an achiever. It is a rare ability and not by any means common. Finding it out becomes the turning point of your destiny. I'm about to take you through a journey; you may never find this in any book. Not even the formal education you receive in your schools and institutions of learning would expose it to you. It's a journey of self discovery where you are going to learn what it takes to have a fulfilled life on earth. By the time you're done reading this book, you'll be flying on the wings of self-belief, motivated by self discovery and leading to inevitable accomplishments. However, I've got Good News for you! You have everything it takes to become a star on the earth. Now join me as we unfold much more.

MAXIMIZING YOUR TALENT

EVERYONE HAS TALENTS

"Wherefore he saith, when he ascended up on high, he led captivity captive, and gave gifts unto men."(Ephesians 4:8) In the verse above, the Apostle emphatically states that everyone has been given gifts or talents from God. Why? For the establishment of a God predetermined agenda! God has plans, but He uses human vessels. Everyone matters to God. You are central to a divine plan. No farmer goes to his farm without his implements. Similarly, God couldn't have sent you down here on missions He hasn't equipped you for. Therefore, you cannot be without gifting, endowments and special abilities. You did not determine where, when and why you were born. God determined all that before your parents even met each other (Jeremiah 1:5). You are born at an appointed time, in an appointed place, with specific gifts to solve well defined problems. Everyone's assignment differs. When I was young, I used to wish I was an American or a European, living in London, New York, etc. Growing up however and discovering more about myself, I can say with every sense of audacity that I'm proud to be a Nigerian, born in Nigeria and Gifted to solve specific problems.

I've studied a bit about Nations. In every Nation, there is a natural resource.

In Nigeria for example, there is Crude Oil, in Ghana, there is Gold. In England, there is Coal. In Germany, there is Uranium, etc. Each Nation draws from its natural resources to produce wealth for its citizenry. Nations differ in wealth depending on the level of utilization of their resources. Similarly, every human being has a gift, a potential, a natural endowment and a special ability.

The level of your success depends on the level of your utilization of that talent. In every discipline and area of Endeavour, there are specialists. In sports, there are talented athletes. If you don't have the gift, don't try to be an athlete by all means. Look out for your own potential. Some people have the voice to sing, some have the personality to encourage, some; the hands to write, some; craft, some; drawing, some; talking, and so on. Know also that it's possible to be endowed with two or three or even as many talents as possible. Some people can do several things perfectly, you almost wonder if they are from another planet.

The Bible said "God is able to make all grace abound to you…" (2 Corinthians 9:8). That means you can have abundance of gifts. 'Benjamin Franklin' was an author, printer, inventor, scientist and politician. 'Leonardo Da Vinci' was not only the best artist of his time; he also came up with ideas for the helicopter tank, solar power, calculator and the theory of plate tectonics. 'Paul Robeson' did not only have a beautiful bass-baritone voice, he was also a great athlete, writer, multi-lingual orator, scholar and lawyer. 'Isaac Newton' was a mathematician, physicist, theologian, astronomer, alchemist and philosopher. 'Albert Schweitzer' was a musician, peace activist, physician, philosopher and theologian. 'Aristotle's' writings covered poetry, metaphysics, logic, physics, music, theatre, politics, biology, ethics and zoology. 'Thomas Jefferson', former president of the United States was an inventor, architect, politician, writer and wine maker. 'Isaac Asimov', having written 500 books and 9000 letters and post cards, said, "Never think that you're not good enough yourself. People will take you at your own reckoning." I can go on and on.

The summary of what I'm saying is that you have a talent and there is a possibility that you have multiple talents that are yet to be discovered.

But it's absolutely impossible for anyone to exist without a talent because everyone has a purpose and there's a resource deposited in you for the fulfillment of your purpose; and that resource is called 'Talent.'

YOUR TALENT IS A POINTER TO YOUR ASSIGNMENT

"For I would, that all men were even as myself. But every man hath his special gift of God; one after this manner and another after that" (1 Corinthians 7:7) You have an assignment. You are not an accidental creature. You are not on earth because your dad met your mum. You were born because an agenda was created and God ordained you to spearhead the accomplishment of that agenda. The talent you have is a resource that God has deposited in you to equip you for the agenda. Cherish your talents, nurture them and deploy them.

Lt. Dr Myles Munroe said in one of his books and I paraphrase; "the cemetery is the richest place on earth." Why?

In my opinion, it's because many people died without discovering, developing and deploying their talents. Apostle Paul in the text above said everyone has his own gift "one after this manner and another after that." That means we all have different talents. My talent differs from yours; because we have different assignments. There's no point trying to copy someone else because your reason for existence differs from everyone else.

That's why when students talk, you hear one person say "I hate Maths"; and then another one says "I love it but I hate Biology." A third person comes in and says "you've got to be kidding, because Geography is my favourite." Everyone has a different ability because everyone has a different destiny; simple! God Works With Varieties Imagine if everybody on earth were musicians; no doctors, no lawyers, no pastors, no teachers, nothing else; just musicians. There would be chaos. When people have a headache, they would die, because no doctor. If everybody was a sportsman, there would be no spectator. If everybody was a preacher, there would be no members. God created several gifts because there are several needs.

There are varieties of gifting. Your own talent is an answer to someone else' need! I Need Yours and You Need Mine Recently I watched a documentary of how the "Burj al Arab" (world tallest hotel) was built in Dubai. Hundreds of millions of dollars went into the project. But there was a variety of skills on display and a lot of professionals in different areas of construction had to come together to make the project work. First, an architect was needed to design the iconic structure, and then engineers in land reclamation were called upon to create an artificial island because the edifice was built a few meters into the ocean, building commenced, brick layers were needed, then electricians, then plumbers, interior decorators, painters, carpenters, and so on. Everyone had a different assignment based on their several abilities. However, they all worked together to make the building stand. Without the brick layer, there would be no structure for the electrician to work on; and without the architect, there would be no idea for the brick layer to implement. It's simple! We all have different abilities, but we need each other. When a teacher is sick, he or she needs a doctor. When a doctor has a child, he needs the teacher to educate the child.

Talents are given to service other people's needs to the glory of God. Copy No One! Many people fail because they try to copy others. I said earlier that you need not copy anyone because you have a unique assignment. It was tagged on your life before you were born. No one else has it. Therefore you don't have to try to be someone else. It's ok to admire endowments you see in others; but focus on developing yours. In the mid 2000's, a number of popular Nigerian actors were banned for a year because they were charging outrageous sums of money to do movies. That year, more than half of them decided to go into music –just to show that they weren't moved by the ban. However, majority of them flopped. They were fantastic actors but woeful singers. Some of them sang   so terribly I felt for them. I heard one of them sing and I actually thought she was coughing.

EVERY GOOD GIFT COMES FROM GOD

"Every good gift and every perfect gift is from above, and cometh down from the father of lights, with whom is no variableness, neither shadow of turning." (James 1:17) "Whatever is good and perfect comes to us from God above who created all heaven's lights; unlike them, He never changes or casts shifting shadows." (James 1:17, NLT) There are good gifts and there are bad gifts. But every good gift comes from God. In fact, everything God deposited in man was good. However, through satanic influences, some people acquire bad gifts from the devil. Jesus explains this better in John 8:44. "Ye are of your father the devil, and the lusts of your father ye will do. He was a murderer from the beginning and abode not in the truth, because there is no truth in him.

When he speaketh a lie, he speaketh of his own, for he is a liar and the father of it" Jesus says the devil is father to certain individuals who will replicate his characteristics –a murderer and a liar. Also, the devil is called the thief and the destroyer in John 10:10. There are people who are gifted liars; but God couldn't have gifted anyone to lie. It must behave come from the devil. It's a bad gift. There are people who are talented thieves; they just pick up anything they see.

They got that from their father –the devil. There are many murderers, destroyers   to make a donation to this author: adulterers and so on. God never gives such gifts to anyone. They're all from the devil, no doubt. Those under the influence of Satan are gifted with bad talents, but those under God's influence exhibit good gifts. It's simple! In 1 John 3:9-10, John the Beloved said "whosoever is born of God does not commit sin…In this, the children of God are manifest, and the children of the devil; whosoever doeth not righteousness is not of God…"The Apostle clearly states that there are Children of God and there are children of the devil. Everyone exhibits the gifting of whom he belongs. With Whom is No Variableness! God is never partial. He gave gifts to all men (Ephesians 4:8); and there is no variableness with his gifts (James 1:17). He doesn't give powerful gifting to some and less important ones to others. Your talent is just as important as anyone else' own. God has no respect for persons (2 Chronicles 19:7b). He's given good gifts to everyone. Your success depends on how you are able to utilize yours.

Romans 9:12 says "…the same lord over all is rich unto all…" Paul wrote in 1 Corinthians 12:4: "Now there are diversities (different types) of gifts, but the same Spirit. And there are different administrations, but the same Lord. And there are diversities of operations, but it is the same God which worketh all in all" (Emphasis mine). Also, "There is One body and One Spirit, even as ye are called in One hope of your calling: One Lord, One faith, One baptism, One God and One Father of all, Click here or copy to make a donation to this author: who is above all and through all and in you all. But unto every one of us is given grace according to the measure of the gift of Christ." (Ephesians 4:4-7). There is a measure of the gift of Christ in everyone; and it is a pointer to each one's destiny. We're in the same Body of Christ but we're given diversities of gifts to function in different areas. These gifts come from God –the Father of lights; with whom is no variableness neither shadow of turning.

YOU ARE EXPECTED TO MAKE PROFIT WITH YOUR TALENT

"But the manifestation of the Spirit is given to every man to profit withal" (1 Corinthians 12:7) Talents are for profit making. They're not mere decorations. In Matthew chapter 25, Jesus told a parable of the master who gave out different amounts of talents to three of his servants prior to his journey. On his return, he rewarded the first two servants who made profits with theirs and punished the third for not making any profit. Remember that talents are given by God to us so we can accomplish certain God-predetermined tasks or assignments (John 15:2). Failure to maximize our talents means we are not making any profits with what he's given us. You are expected to produce results with what you've been given. You are gifted to affect both yourself and humanity positively. A few years back, a Russian billionaire bought two pieces of artwork from an American painter for 200 million dollars. My jaws dropped when the news broke out. I began to wonder whether there was a piece of diamond hiding somewhere in the painting; but there was none. It was just an outstanding artwork that cost so much. The truth is; there are many other talented painters who are not deploying their gifting;

hence, there's no profit whatsoever for them. Recently, a popular soccer player in England said "what we earn in this profession   is crazy compared to what we obtain in normal life."

Many of us live in   a mundane existence in which we get up, go to work, come home, and go to sleep. This cycle keeps repeating each and every day. The worst part is that we likely work a job that we don't enjoy doing, but we keep working that job in order to provide for our family. Stop right now and pay attention, because it doesn't have to be that way. This book; Stir Up the Gift Within, encourages people to use their talents to do what they love. It teaches people exactly how to find their talents so that they can use them to pursue their passions in life. There are bigger dreams and goals lurking inside each and every one of us; we need to stir up that gift within us. The difference between successful people and ordinary people is that successful people take action and pursue their dreams. Ordinary people tend to accept what life has thrown at them without trying to make any changes or go against the ideals of society in order to seek out that better life. All successful people found a way to use their talents to do what they love. The hardest part was learning how to do it, and that is exactly what you will learn in this book.

Therefore I remind you to stir up the gift of God which is in you through the laying on of my hands. For God has not given us a spirit of fear, but of power and of love and of a sound mind." (2 Timothy 1:6-7) "God gives food to every bird, but doesn't throw them in the nest." – Unknown author Every one of us has a personal responsibility for their spiritual gifts received by God. By this I don't mean to touch on how to recognize which gifts we have from God, or the source of those gifts, rather I mean personal responsibility to those gifts, Although these gifts are "free" and given by God for the building up of the church, from what we know in 1st Corinthians, where Paul breaks down the spiritual gifts for us, we ought not to take them lightly and we carry a responsibility to stir them up so that they function and are effective in Christ's body for building up the church so that God is glorified and His work extended. Although these gifts are "free" and given by God for the building up of the church, ought not to take them lightly and we carry a responsibility to stir them

     THE POWER OF POSITIVE MIND

up so that they function and are effective in Christ's body for building up the church so that God is glorified and His work extended.

1. EACH ONE OF US HAS GOD'S GIFTS FOR WHICH WE ARE RESPONSIBLE.

"Therefore I remind you to stir up the gift of God which is in you through the laying on of my hands." (1 Timothy 1:6) Paul was telling Timothy to stir up his own gift of God that he received as a result of the laying on of his [Paul's] hands on him. The gift here is not described, but without a doubt we can say that the gift came to Timothy as a result of his being sent forth into the ministry of evangelism. We know this from 1st Timothy, in which he also told Timothy to not neglect the gift that was in him: "Do not neglect the gift that is in you, which was given to you by prophecy with the laying on of the hands of the eldership." (1 Timothy 4:14) Therefore, God's gift was found in Timothy according to his personal responsibility. We see the magnitude of personal responsibility needed in the first and second letters to Timothy, especially in the second, which is actually his last letter written before his death. In his letters Paul wanted to pass on the torch to the next generation of leaders coming after him, as to all believers in general. Among other things, he emphasized personal responsibility to our spiritual gifts. If we carefully examine this we will note that in the first letter to Timothy he says to not neglect the gift and in the second to stir up the gift. The word stir up literally means to blow upon or blow upon dying embers so the fire blazes once again. Each one of us has one or more spiritual gifts for which we are personally responsible to God. They can be used for His glory and His kingdom. Many times Jesus Christ spoke about personal responsibility for those things we have received, He spoke about this as our Christian duty. For this reason I would like to look at the parable in regards to personal responsibility for what we have received, which is found in Matthew 25. Jesus spoke about the talents entrusted to certain servants in order to show us our personal responsibility for them. "And to one he gave five talents, to another two, and to another one, to each according to his own ability; and immediately he went on a journey. " (Matthew 25:15) So the master (Jesus) divided the money (talents) among his servants (believers) according to their ability. No one received more or less than they were able to bear, so that if a servant did not manage his responsibility he could not blame it on the fact that he could not manage. Our personal failures have no connection with whether or not we have too much or too little, rather because we are simply too lazy or have animosity toward our Master. The talents in this story represent every kind of resource, which we personally possess. Each one of us has one or more spiritual gifts for which we are personally responsible to God. They can be used for His glory and His kingdom.

 God has given us time, gifts, finances, and other resources according to our ability and He expects us to wisely invest them until His second coming. Therefore, we are responsible for that which God has entrusted us. It's not so much about how much we possess, rather whether or not we use wisely what we have. The rest of the story is familiar to us; there are useful and ineffective servants, those who utilized and multiplied their gifts and received more, and those who were lazy and despised their master. Everything was taken from them and they were thrown into hell. "And cast the unprofitable servant into the outer darkness. There will be weeping and gnashing of teeth." (Matthew 25:30) Although Paul encouraged Timothy and implored him to give his all for the Lord, Timothy also had to be responsible not to neglect his spiritual gift received by God and to stir it up. This was not an option; rather he was imperatively challenged to do so. Let us look at some of those imperative words Paul used in relation to his gift in both of the letters sent to Timothy: "Do not neglect; stir up the gift; this charge I commit to you; keep the faith; reject profane and old wives' tales; for we are laboring and fighting; be an example; give attention to reading, exhortation and doctrine; pursue righteousness, faith, love, perseverance, gentleness; fight the good fight of faith; I urge you… keep this commandment without spot, blameless; guard what is committed to your trust; be strong in the grace…" I want to emphasize that we are all personally responsible for the gifts and resources that we have received from God, which is why we cannot just passively expect a power from on high to touch and activate us. We simply must actively begin to stir up the gifts and not neglect that which we have received from the Lord. We ought not to allow ourselves to be lulled into religiosity and lethargy. In order to be fruitful we must act on our own because Jesus is coming soon and will seek from us an account of every gift, every resources, and all that we have received of Him; all that we have received and all that we have is not meant only for our own use, rather for His kingdom.

2. WE CAN STIR UP THE GIFTS WITHOUT FEAR OF THE PAST, PRESENT AND FUTURE.

"For God has not given us a spirit of fear, but of power and of love and of a sound mind." (2 Timothy 1:7)

Paul further encourages Timothy to stir up the God has given us time, gifts, finances, and other resources according to our ability and He expects us to wisely invest them until His second coming. We are responsible for that which God has entrusted us. It's not so much about how much we possess, rather whether or not we use wisely what we have such as   spiritual gift from God without fear and writes that God did not give him a spirit of fear. The Greek word for "fear" that Paul uses here is deilia, which we translate: "cowardice, reticence, or fears". Usually this word was used in a negative context when compared to the Greek word phobos, the word for fear which perhaps came from the word peophoba, indicating idea of fleeing from something. In other words, Paul is telling Timothy that God did not give him a spirit of cowardice, reticence, and fear that causes us to flee and pull away from the Lord and those things that He has for us through gifts and talents with which He has entrusted us. I am personally convinced that many Christians have ceased growing spiritually and are no longer spiritually productive, other than attending church, because of bad personal experiences in the past. I believe that in the beginning of their conversion many were open and powerful in faith and in God's gifts. They gave of their time and finances and were open to spiritual things until a moment in their walk with Jesus when they had a bad experience while serving in their gifts; because of an offense they became skeptical, doubtful and fearful. Actually, in these moments of disappointment, if we are not careful, that spirit of fear can come on us, paralyze and terrify us so that we no longer advance in faith and optimism as before. And what happens then? Because of the devilish opposition that we have faced in those moments of surrender to the Lord, because people have disappointed us, and we have experienced negative circumstances, we decide to pull into ourselves, lay aside the gifts we have received and, rather than being the productive, positive believer we once were, we become embittered, doubtful, cynical, selfish, and frightened; we are so introverted that we can no longer receive from the Lord that which He has for us, nor can we serve others. We no longer move forward toward the future because we live in fear of further failure and disappointment. So we choose to stop, which is not healthy for us or for Christ's body. Timothy also experienced great opposition, personally and as a leader. His youth, connection with Paul, and leadership went through fiery attack from believers and unbelievers alike. This is why Paul urged him to be brave. Had Timothy allowed people or the devil to frighten him, his effectiveness would have been neutralized; which is why the power of the Holy Spirit is needed so we can overcome the fear of man. Maybe we are not like Paul, but the past can neutralize our effectiveness cause us to be Jesus is coming soon and will seek from us an account of every gift, every resources, and all that we have received of Him; all that we have received and all that we have is not meant only for our own use, rather for His kingdom led by fear. In this case our thoughts will be filled with questions such as "What do I do now? Where can I run? Where can I hide? How will I overcome?" The spirit of fear can only be conquered by God's Spirit, this is also how we stir up His resources in us. We cannot simply complain and wait for better days, thinking that with time things will right themselves.

We must pull ourselves together and act, knowing what we have in God. This is why Paul continued on by saying that God did not give us a spirit of fear but of "power, love, and of a sound mind". (2 Timothy 1:7b) Let us quickly look at what kind of spirit God gave us. First of all, a spirit of power. For the word power Paul used the Greek word dunamis, which literally means "might". This word is especially used in the context of inverted power, for example in the case when Jesus felt the power go out of Him when the woman with the issue of blood for twelve years touched His garment. When she touched Him, the blood immediately stopped flowing and she was healed. "And Jesus, immediately knowing in Himself that power had gone out of Him." (Mark 5:30a) We find this same word in Ephesians when Paul spoke about greatness of God's power in us. "…and what [is] the exceeding greatness of His power toward us who believe, according to the working of His mighty power." (Ephesians 1:19) All the words derived from the root word duna have the basic meaning of "to have capability or to be able". In other words, Paul says that God alone has enabled and equipped us to get out of the pit of self-pity, the fear of man, the fear of repeated failure, and hurt and to stir up the gift that God has given us without fear of the past, present or future – because God has given us the spirit of power to overcome all things! Second, Paul said that God has given us, in addition to the spirit of power, a spirit of love. The word agape actually depicts the benevolence, charity, and compassion of God's love. This love is not made up of what we want as objects of love, rather of that which the one who loves us believes is most needful. In other words, God didn't give us what we wanted, rather what He thought we needed – His Son who brought us salvation from sin. This is God's love (agape) for us, that which He thinks is best for us. His agape love is willfully directed toward each man, but in order for man to show his love for God he must first accept God's agape love, because only God has this kind of unselfish love. Therefore, Paul tells Timothy that God has give him His spirit of love that will willfully direct him to unselfishness and love, and that will, then, manifest in stirring up of The spirit of fear can only be conquered by God's Spirit, this is also how we stir up His resources in us. We cannot simply complain and wait for better days, thinking that with time things will right themselves.

3. BY BEARING FRUITS AND WATCHING OVER THEM

 stir up   his gifts and in bearing good fruit for His kingdom. By accepting this kind of love we become motivated and furthermore remain motivated in this unselfish kind of love that will not leave us barren and paralyzed in our selfish lives. This kind of love will not leave us bound in chains of the past, because it is an unselfish love that always gives of itself regardless of opposition, hurt, and rejection. Let us remember Christ's unselfish love and prayer. Jesus, filled with this kind of love, despite hurts, rejection, and opposition from people, on the cross of Golgotha, was able to go on, forgive, and die for them. "Then Jesus said, 'Father, forgive them, for they do not know what they do." (Luke 23:34a) This kind of spirit always gives us strength to once again stir up the gifts and all that God has entrusted to us, regardless of the past, present or future. We do not have to live in fear of hurt, disappointment, and hardship; hurt, disappointment and hardship will come to all of us, but with Christ we can overcome and go on. Thirdly, Paul told us that God gave us a spirit of a sound mind. Some translations use the word "wise discretion". The Greek word that Paul used for "sound mind" was sophronismos. This word comes from the word sophronizo that literally conveys the idea of "calling to soundness of mind". Figuratively it means to discipline or correct, to teach someone how to be sober, healthy, restrained of mind. In other words, Paul says that it is possible to continue on because God has enabled us to have retrained, wise, and healthy thoughts that will help us in stirring up the gifts and resources God has given us. I want to emphasize something else that is very important. Often in the Greek language when it speaks about a certain spirit the word indicates more of an attitude or an actual spirit. Therefore, the encouragement Paul was giving Timothy, as well as all of us, was that we do not need to fear because we have a promise from God and God has given us a different spirit or an attitude different than that of this world. Paul told us to freely stir up the gift that is in us. This is the attitude that every new believer should have: courage, love, and a sound mind. An attitude that does not fear the past, present or future; it is a spirit that is productive, positive, and full of faith; a spirit that gives of itself regardless of a difficult past, momentary difficult circumstances, or perhaps a doubtful future.

4. THEREFORE, LET'S LEARN SOMETHING BY APPLYING LOVE AND SACRIFICE TO AID HUMANITY

"Therefore do not be ashamed of the testimony of our Lord, nor of me His prisoner, but share with me in the sufferings for the gospel according to the power of Agape depicts the benevolence, charity, and compassion of God's love. This love is not made up of what we want as objects of love, rather of that which the one who loves us believes is most needful. (2 Timothy 1:8) In that day of persecution and difficulties, Timothy was afraid to continue preaching the gospel. His fears were well founded. Believers around him were imprisoned and killed. Paul told Timothy to expect difficulty. Actually, Timothy, like Paul, was imprisoned for preaching the gospel. This is clearly seen in Hebrews when the writer in the end gave information about Timothy's freedom saying, "Know that [our] brother Timothy has been set free, with whom I shall see you if he comes shortly." (Hebrews 13:23) Nevertheless, Paul promised Timothy that God would give him strength and to be ready for when trouble came. Even when there is no persecution it can be very difficult to share our faith in Christ. Yet, thank God, like Paul and Timothy, we can have God's strength to stir up His gifts. This is why it is good for us to learn this now. If we wait for a spontaneous stirring up of the fire then it will simply burn out. As for fire, when we notice that it is starting to wane it is best to stir it up immediately. God wants us to stir up His resources and gifts courageously in agape love and with a sound mind. But, how do we do this? Should we expect something mysterious or is it something we ought to do ourselves? We already know the answer – much of it depends on us, our actions, and our attitudes. Paul went on to give Timothy practical and helpful advise in "stirring up God's gifts". We see, for example, once again, Paul's imperative and practical instructions to Timothy to stir up the gifts. He didn't tell him to pray, sit, and wait for a special day of revival, although this ought to be done every day by every believer. Rather, he clearly instructed him with several instructions for what he could immediately begin doing. Let us look at the some of the examples of these imperative statements. "Therefore, do not be ashamed of the testimony of our Lord, nor of me His prisoner." (2 Timothy 1:8a), "…share with me in the sufferings for the gospel according to the power of God." (2 Timothy 1:8b). "That good thing that was committed to you,

     THE POWER OF POSITIVE MIND

keep by the Holy Spirit who dwells in us" (2 Timothy 1:14), "…be strong in the grace that is in Christ Jesus", "commit these to faithful men", "endure hardship as a good soldier of Jesus Christ", Remember… Jesus Christ", Remind [them] of these things, charging [them] before the Lord", "Be diligent to present yourself approved to God", "Flee also youthful lusts", "But avoid foolish and ignorant disputes". (2 Timothy 2:1c, 2a, 3, 8a, 14a, 15a, 22a, 23a) These were specific things that Timothy needed to do in order to stir up the gift, or gifts, that he received from the Lord. What this means for us is dependent upon our situation. We have a personal responsibility. Perhaps in the beginning, for some of us, to By accepting this kind of love we become motivated and furthermore remain motivated in this unselfish kind of love that will not leave us barren and paralyzed in our selfish lives.

5. STIR UP THE GIFT OF GOD BY   GIVING A HELPING SHOULDER FOR ANOTHER

stir up means to not neglect getting up in the morning for personal devotions. Maybe this means to knock on a neighbor's door, invite him to coffee, and share the gospel with him. Possibly it means to take up an instrument and play for the Lord, grab some tracts and share them on the street, begin to write a book, begin to preach, clean, strengthen your ministry, feed a hungry neighbor, turn off the television and computer and rest for a while, forgive those who have hurt you and do something nice for them. Maybe it means to change our bad attitude and become positive, or to return to a ministry in which you once served. Perhaps for some this means to surrender your finances to the Lord, lend to those in need, or perhaps simply to give your full tithe to the church. There are many things that we can do without fear of the past, present and future, without fear of hurt, failure, or disappointment, because we must know that God has not given us a spirit of fear, but of power, love and a sound mind. With that spirit, or with that attitude, our gifts will be stirred up and multiplied for Him in praise and glory. When Jesus comes, we will be able to say without fear, "'Lord, you delivered to me five talents; look, I have gained five more talents besides them." And He will say to us, "Well [done], good and faithful servant; you were faithful over a few things, I will make you ruler over many things. Enter into the joy of your lord." (Matthew 25: 20b-21) Therefore, let us stir up our resources and gifts; this is our responsibility. There are many things that we can do without fear of the past, present and future, without fear of hurt, failure, or disappointment, because we must know that God has not given us a spirit of fear, but of power, love and a sound mind

So may be you are stuck in the crowd   With constant peer pressure from social media to define yourself   , it's no surprise that who you *actually* are gets lost in the shuffle.

But once you get away from those glowing screens of identity-makers, you will be able to utilize and maximize your potentials and talents and gifts .

How do we decide what our strengths are and how to use them?

Identify your talents and start using them now with these ten simple tips:

1. Take a personality test.

Think these tests are a one size fits all approach? Think again. Personality tests are an objective way of understanding what makes you tick. The <u>Meyers-Briggs Type Indicator</u> is a popular tool to help you define the patterns in your seemingly complex personality. Once you know which category you fall into, you can start seeing your strengths and weaknesses more clearly in everyday life. Use this to your advantage by walking into a job interview, first date or any other high stakes situation and playing to your newly discovered strengths.

2. Find what makes you feel strong.

Ever have those moments when everything feels easy and light? You know that you have the answer or are capable of finding the answer? When we are drawn toward a sense of ease that is usually our inner talent scout speaking up. Notice when you feel your strongest and create more opportunities to feel that way. If you're naturally good with kids, see if you can volunteer time at an after school program or babysit for a friend who needs a little help. Let your strengths lead your schedule.

3. Find what you spend the most money on.

We often put our money where our mouth is when it comes to what we desire. Using easy and free applications like <u>Mint</u> to go back through your finances is a great way to notice where you pour your dollars. When you follow the green you discover what you value, and chances are you have a knack for what you value. If you go back through your yearly spending and notice that your biggest expense is that group fitness class you love, use that as a sign of your athleticism. Sign up for a road race, try a new kind of class or simply just commit to a healthy lifestyle

S

4. Ask your friends what your best and worst qualities are.

You know they are going to be brutally honest. But the great thing about asking a handful of trusted friends about your qualities is that they all usually say the same thing. It's enlightening to hear different people see you in the same light and this is definitely an indicator of talent. Use your friends' perspectives here to work on what you'd like to do better. Are you compassionate but also a little bit on the chatty side? Use your compassion to slow down, breathe and give others the right of conversational way. Use your natural talents to improve those parts of your M.O. that might need a little work.

5. Ask your family what you loved as a child.

Sometimes the people who have known us the longest are the people who know us the best. Ask your family what you used to do as a kid – maybe you always played alone, with friends, made up stories, wrote, drew, acted out scenes, played baseball, read books. More than likely these are things you still love today, but some things we easily forget as we grow into responsible, mature, serious adults. Take these recollections as a hint to get busy playing again. See how much of your childhood you can recreate in your adulthood by following your sense of play. Using your talents in recreation gives your brain a chance to play, making you more productive in every other area of your life.

6. Write in a journal.

Let your thoughts flow onto a few pages every morning and walk away from them for the rest of the day. Stream of consciousness writing can be very effective at identifying your talents. Come back after a week and re-read your pages. You'll notice a lot of your thoughts circle back to one main idea. This is usually a talent or desire. Use your writing to look for hidden answers. What are you missing? What are you longing for? What opportunities do you wish would come through? Then, use your journal to create a list of your strengths and a list of opportunities to set new goals that are aligned with those strengths.

7. Look for talent in others.

Sometimes being inspired by others' talents makes us realize what we're good at, too. If you are a writer and you read something that absolutely connects with your soul, try to define what exactly lit you up. Conversely, if you see talent in others and feel jealous (don't you worry, we *all* do this) you can use this to your advantage as well. Ask this person to mentor you, give you advice or simply chat over coffee. Reaching out and seeing talent in others will open up opportunities and connections while helping you define your own.**Reach My Goa**

8. Take stock of your book/music/movie collections.

The media we consume says a lot about what we value, but what we own says something even larger. This is a true identity maker. I am extremely aware of what books I read on the subway because I know that I'm outwardly identifying something hidden about myself on my morning commute. Glance through all of your collections, what is the one resonating idea? This is probably something that lights your fire. Dig further into this, is there a convention, a class, a workshop you could take to use this talent? How can you connect with others who enjoy the same thing as you? All of these avenues lead to connections and potential networking, so go ahead with your talented self.

9. Remember what you have been thanked for.

When people thank us for something, they have been helped in some way. Notice what you are thanked for on the regular. Are you a good listener? A good teacher? A good motivator? All of these things are talents even though they seem small. Remember that your talents shouldn't just be in service to other people, but to you as well. If you're in a constant mode of selflessness, use your talent as a caregiver to take care of yourself. Know that as you give to yourself, you're growing your ability to give to others.

10. Be open to change.

Know that as we age, our tastes change and our strengths grow. Don't allow yourself to be complacent by telling yourself the same story over and over again. If you say, *I'm not athletic because I didn't play sports in high school*, you're not giving your current self a chance to identify new talents. Being open to change means letting go of preconceived notions and honestly absorbing the world around you. This kind of openness will lead you to discover new talents and help prepare you to tackle any challenge life throws your way.

What You Say In Difficult Time Does Matter:

A lesson from a pilot on to   brace up your potentials mentally

A pilot study from North Carolina State University finds that people are not consistent in how they prepare mentally to deal with arguments and other stressors, with each individual displaying a variety of coping behaviors.

In addition, the study found that the coping strategies people used could affect them the following day.

The findings stem from a pilot study of older adults, which is the first to track the day-to-day coping behaviors people use in advance of stressful events.

"This finding tells us, for the first time, that these behaviors are dynamic," says Dr. Shevaun Neupert, lead author of a paper describing the study and an associate professor of psychology at NC State. "This highlights a whole new area for researching the psychology of daily health and well-being.

"And these are behaviors that can be taught," Neupert adds. "The more we understand what's really going on, the better we'll be able to help people deal effectively with the stressors that come up in their lives."

To learn more about how older adults prepare themselves mentally ahead of stressful events, the researchers developed a pilot study of 43 adults between the ages of 60 and 96.

Participants were asked to fill out a daily questionnaire on their activities and feelings -- including whether anything stressful had happened -- on the current day. Participants were also asked to predict whether they expected there to be a stressful event the following day, and how they were preparing for it. The participants were asked to complete the questionnaire on eight consecutive days. The researchers ultimately had data on 380 days, since some participants missed reporting days.

"The reporting was done using very specific questions with clearly defined metrics, such as ranking how stressed they felt on a scale of one to five," Neupert explains. The questionnaires also asked participants the extent to which they were engaging in specific behaviours associated with coping with upcoming potential stressors.

The results found that people used different coping behaviours to prepare for different stressors, and that those coping behaviours changed from day to day.

"The findings tell us that one person may use multiple coping mechanisms over time -- something that's pretty exciting since we didn't know this before," Neupert says. "But we also learned that what you do on Monday really makes a difference for how you feel on Tuesday."

Some anticipatory coping behaviours, particularly outcome fantasy and stagnant deliberation, were associated with people being in worse moods and reporting more physical health problems the following day. Stagnant deliberation is when someone tries, unsuccessfully, to solve a problem. Outcome fantasy is when someone wishes that problem would effectively solve itself.

However, stagnant deliberation was also associated with one positive outcome. Namely, stagnant deliberation the day before an argument was correlated with fewer memory failures after the argument.

The researchers also looked at plan rehearsal and problem analysis as anticipatory coping strategies. Plan rehearsal involves mentally envisioning the steps needed to solve the potential problem, and problem analysis is actively thinking about the source and meaning of a future problem. The researchers found that the use of these strategies changed from day to day, but the changes in these strategies were not related to well-being the next day. They were also not related to the way that people responded to arguments the next day.

"This was a pilot study, so we don't want to get carried away," Neupert says. "But these findings are very intriguing. They raise a lot of questions, and we're hoping to follow up with a much larger study."

In summary , it doesn't matter how many times you have being confused about your gifts or talents and not even in how many mistakes you have made nor countless times you must have failed , as far as you can   get back to your feet again and dust of yourself from the   ground , and search deeply into you , without comparing yourself to another , I bet you you will fly with you gift and you will be celebrated .

Chapter Eight

FEW NUGGETS TO REVIEW ABOUT THE
MIND

1 .What Are You Picturing In Your Mind?

"I had a baseball coach once who always said, "Whatever you do Bassham, don't strike out." What do you picture when I say, "Don't strike out." It is impossible to think about hitting the ball if you are picturing striking out."

"It is impossible to picture winning and losing at the same time. You are either picturing something that will help you or something that will hurt you."

According to Lanny, it doesn't really matter which words we use when we think or talk.
What matters is the picture that gets created
in our minds. Think about it:

What happens when I say, "Don't think about a

pink elephant?" Damn right, your mind pictures a

pink elephant.

What happens when you're about to hit the ball and you or someone
else is constantly telling you, "Don't strike out! Don't strike out!
Don't strike out!"
Yep, you picture yourself NOT hitting the ball, but

striking out instead. This is HUGELY important.

We have to take control over our mental pictures.

Everything we're picturing either helps us and moves us in the right direction or harms us and moves us in the wrong direction.

Just like every action and every decision you make… every mental picture you create in your mind either helps you achieve your goals or moves you further away from your goals.

(**Note:** It doesn't matter who creates the picture in your mind. It could be your coach, your mother, your friends, or yourself. What matters is the picture that gets created. Keep that in mind.)

2. The Mental Picture Is Formed By What You Think, Talk, Or Write About

"Our conscious picture is formed from what you think about, talk about, and write about.

Let's keep this short and simple:

The conscious picture is formed from what we think about, talk

about, and write about. (Or, as I mentioned earlier, by what

someone else talks to you about.)

So controlling your mental pictures happens by controlling what you think, talk, and write about.

Simple enough.

Let's go one step further.

3 .Be Careful What You ~~Wish For~~ Picture

"The more we think about, talk about, and write about something happening, we improve the probability of that thing happening!"
Now it gets real interesting.

Every time you think about, talk about, or write about something happening (--> you picture something in your mind), you increase the odds of that thing happening.

Are you constantly telling yourself that you'll fail a certain exam? Well congrats! Every time you do that, you improve the probability of failing the exam.

Are you telling yourself that you'll miss the crucial penalty kick? Too bad! Every time you do that, you improve the probability of missing that penalty kick.

Lanny calls this reinforcement.

Every time you create a picture in your mind, you reinforce that picture and increase the likelihood of making it a reality.

You can either use positive reinforcement (great idea!) or negative reinforcement (terrible idea!).

Let's further examine this…

3. Positive Reinforcement

This is when you reinforce a positive behavior.

Remember that the more we think about, talk about, and write about something happening, the higher the probability of that thing happening.

When you reinforce a positive behavior, you increase the likelihood of that behavior happening again.

    a. Hit a grand slam? Reinforce it.
    b. Just meditated for 20 minutes? Reinforce it.
    c. Had a great study session without being distracted? Reinforce it.

d. Ate a healthy meal? Reinforce it.
e. Just exercised? Reinforce it.
f. Finished a work project? Reinforce it.
g. Won a game?

Reinforce it. The point is:

Whenever you do something beneficial, you want to reinforce it.

Because reinforcing it improves the likelihood of that thing

happening again. Sooo that begs the question:

How do you positively reinforce

something? By thinking, talking,

or writing about it.

Here are some ways to do it:

h. Praise yourself ("I did that really well. That's like me.")
i. Praise someone else ("You absolutely rocked this. Greatly
   done!")
j. Write down 5 wins at the end of every day
k. Talk about your good behaviour/performance with your friends
   or family

We'll see one awesome strategy Lanny Bassham uses to positively
reinforce something.

5. Negative Reinforcement

   THE POWER OF POSITIVE MIND

"Be careful not to complain. I often hear people, in business as well as sport, complaining about their circumstances. Complaining is negative reinforcement. I teach my students not to reinforce a bad shot by getting angry. Do not reinforce a bad day at the offi

ce by complaining to your spouse. Remember something that you did well each day instead. Fill your thoughts only with your best performances and you cannot help but be successful!"

Ugh… Negative reinforcement its very terrible .

Yet, funny enough, it's what most of us are absolute pros at.

Do something right and nobody gives a sh*t. (= no positive reinforcement.)

Do something wrong and people are all over you telling you what a loser you are andblablabla. (= negative reinforcement.)

Ourselves, we are often the worst offenders. Somehow we were just never taught to reinforce our good behaviors, but instead we were taught to get down on us when we didsomething wrong.
Anyway, it's obvious that we want to reinforce our good

behaviors, not our bad ones. So what are some ways we negatively

reinforce our bad behaviors?

- we talk about our bad performances
- someone else talks about our bad performances
- we complain
- someone else complains
- we get angry at a bad behavior
- we tell ourselves that we're idiots for a certain

bad behaviorRemember:

Every time you think, talk, or write about a bad performance/behavior/whatever, you improve the probability of having another bad performance/behavior/whatever just like itin the future.

Just look what Lanny Bassham says about his toughest competitors:

"One thing I especially remember about training with them was that

they never talkedabout their failures in front of me.

If Wigger (World and Olympic Champion) had a problem, he kept it to himself.

Jack Writer (World and Olympic Champion) was a talker. It was not that Jack bragged on himself, although I can understand how those who didn't know him would think that. Jack just liked to talk. His favorite subject was shooting, and he was his favorite shooter. No matter how many low scores he shot, Jack would only talk about the high ones. The important lesson here is that Writer never reinforced a bad performance and rarely shot a low score in a big match.

Margaret Murdoch (World and Olympic Silver Medalist) rarely talked at all. If she did, it was to compliment others on their performance. I wonder if she knew that every time she praised another shooter, she also improved her own chances of winning?"

The point is:

The top athletes do NOT negatively reinforce their

bad performances. And neither should you.

And neither should I.

6. Catch Yourself Doing Something Right

*"Stop catching yourself doing things wrong and trying to find out why
you are failing. Instead, only think about your successes, never your
failures. An example is the golfer. The mentally uninformed golfer hits
a good shot and says, "Well, I guess I just got lucky that time." When
he hits a bad shot he says, "Why do I always do that?" The mentally*

informed golfer hits a bad shot. He knows it is bad, but says, "Next time I will hit a better shot." Then he hits a good shot and says, "That's a good shot. What did I do right?" See the difference?"

First of all, congratulations!

You're now part of an exclusive club of the mentally informed. Welcome. May you enjoy your stay with us, positively reinforce your good actions, forget about the bad ones, and live a great and enjoyable life.

Seriously, though, this whole positive vs. negative reinforcement stuff was a big epiphany for me.

Instead of catching ourselves doing something wrong, let's from now on catch ourselves doing something right and improve our chances of repeating that positive behavior in the future.

You can catch yourself doing anything right.

Be it cleaning your room, studying, reading, meditating, being kind to someone, having fun, practicing something… whatever it is:

Catch yourself and pat yourself on

the back. Applaud yourself.

Better yet, celebrate yourself.

I know it's counter-intuitive, but that's because our society is seriously messed up. We're all programmed to focus on the negative, to complain, to make excuses, to behave like little bitches, and to use negative reinforcement. Let's stop that.

Instead be nice to yourself and others, focus on the positive, talk about the good things in life, and positively reinforce them.

7. Have   A Mental Rehearsal

"In mental rehearsal you are picturing what you want to see happen

before you actually perform. You go over in your mind exactly how

you want your performance to be conducted. In rifle shooting, you

picture holding the rifle, looking through the sights, centering the

target, and firing the shot in the ten ring. The more vivid the picture,

the better the outcome. The more often you rehearse, the better the chance for success.'' Mental rehearsal is simply visualizing your performance or behavior in your mind.

You can mentally rehearse giving a speech, shooting a free-throw, hitting a grand slam,

writing an exam, or

anything else. The benefits

are threefold:

1) **You are practicing:** Mental rehearsal is mental practice. Maybe it's not as good as actually practicing, but Lanny says it's a great substitute when actual training is not possible due to weather, injury, or time limitations.

2) **No negative reinforcement:** Because you only rehearse good performances, there is no negative reinforcement. It's 100% purely positive reinforcement (which is almost impossible during actual training).

3) **It reduces fear:** This is neat. When you've been in a stressful situation often, the stressor fear you encounter diminishes over time. (Think about the first speech you've ever made. I bet you were more nervous than in your 10th speech, right?) Rehearsal reduces fear because it gives you mental experience in a pressure situation. Lanny claims that he's competed in the Olympic Games twice physically, but thousands of times mentally. Hah, what a legend.

Keep in mind that you mentally rehearse the process of your performance, NOT the outcome. Merely imagining a positive outcome would be counterproductive as I explain in this article.

Anyway, want to see an awesome example that combines mental rehearsal with positive reinforcement? Here you go…

8. Practice like me" Rehearsal + Reinforcement

Rehearse that you're the Greatest.

"You can imagine far more than you currently can achieve. If you consistently rehearse what you want to achieve, what you imagine can become reality. Let me give you an example. Back in the 1970s, I was shooting good kneeling scores and began approaching the national record of 396/400. I wanted to set the record at 400, a perfect score. But I

     THE POWER OF POSITIVE MIND

had never actually fired a 400, even in training. Nonetheless, I vividly rehearsed shooting the first 100, then another and another. I visualized each of the last ten shots building toward the record. I rehearsed what I knew would happen at that point: I would realize

that I was above the record. Next, I rehearsed hearing a voice say, "That's OK. I do this all the time." Then I imagined shooting the final ten easily and saying to myself, "Another 400, that's like me." I rehearsed this sequence several times a day for two months. In my first competition since beginning the rehearsal, I started with a 100 kneeling. My next two targets were also 100s. I began my last series with ten, ten, ten, ten, ten. Only five more to go. Ten. Ten. Ten. Then reality set in. I was above the record. I heard an internal voice say, "That's OK, I do this all the time." I shot two additional tens, setting the national record at a perfect 400."

Did you read this?

No? Do it.

Yes? Awesome, huh?

So he basically mentally rehearsed shooting a perfect record of 400/400.

And when (in his mind) he hit the 400/400 he positively reinforced it by saying, "That's like me" and "I do this all the time."

He's reprogramming his mind and tells it over and over and over again that hitting a perfect 400/400 is "like him" and that he "does it all the time".

Mad cool.

Oh, and he had never even actually shot a 400/400. Not even in training. But of course he then did it straight away in the next competition after using this mental rehearsal + positive reinforcement technique. Just. Like. That.

A BRIEF REVIEW OF THE NUGGETS..

Let's recap this goodness:

First off, you have to take control over what you picture in your mind. Because whenever you picture something in your mind, you increase the likelihood of that thing happening in the future.

You control the picture in your mind (and thus what's happening in the future) by choosing what you think, talk, and write about.

At any given time, you are either picturing something positive or something negative in your mind. You are either thinking, talking, or writing about something positive or you are thinking, talking, or writing about something negative.

In other words, you are reinforcing

certain behaviors. There are two kinds of

reinforcement:

1. **Positive Reinforcement (YES!):** You reinforce something you did well such as hitting a grand slam, meditating, studying, being nice to someone, or whatever. Reinforcing this positive action makes happening it again in the future more likely.
2. **Negative Reinforcement (Meh!):** You reinforce something you did poorly such as missing a shot, wasting time on Facebook, getting in an argument with someone, or whatever. Reinforcing the negative action makes happening it again in the future more likely.
(NOT what we're after!)

Remember:

You reinforce something by thinking, talking, or

writing about it. Let's get real specific now…

<u>How to use positive reinforcement in your life (do this more often!)</u>
- Praise, applaud, and celebrate yourself
- Praise, applaud, and celebrate others (creates the same mental pictures)
- Talk about the positive things in your life (what went well in your life?)
- Get in the habit of catching yourself doing something right (and then praise yourself and tell yourself that "that's like you" and that you "do this all the time"

<u>How to STOP using negative reinforcement in your life (stop doing this!)</u>
- Never whine, bitch, or complain
- Don't listen to other people whining, bitching, or complaining

     THE POWER OF POSITIVE MIND

- Don't get angry about your negative actions
- Don't think/talk about the negative things

in your life And that's it!

The bottom line is: Stop focusing on the negative. Stop complaining, making excuses, bitching around, or in any other way negatively reinforcing what you don't want in life.

Instead be nice to yourself and others, focus on the positive, talk about the good things in   - life and just generally try to reinforce what you want more of in life.

Chapter Nine

WISE WORDS FROM THE AUTHOR'S TABLE

1. Nothing provokes stability of life like absolute obedience to God
2. Each time you encounter a fresh light from the word of God , you knock out the night of your current and future negative situation .

3.Distance doesn't separate people.... silence does …..
4. The size of your vision for kingdom expansion will determine the size of your provision from the king .
5. Lots of single guys are busy looking for Rehanna with a touch of chioma Jesus for a wife .
6. God makes deposits where He is free to make demands without restrictions .
7. In the kingdom of dominion , it is fraudulent to seek for rewards without value and productivity .
8. Any lady who places a price tag above her content will always attract a bad buyer
9. When brutality , incessant killings and injustice to lives gets to its climax , the earth and heaven opens up …
10. Consistency in character and content is a proof that you are

living by a principle

11. Your content may attract multitudes , but only your wisdom will attract kings and queens

12. Lift up your eyes to the sky, for there is hope for our nation

Nigeria , happy 60th independence .

13. Love is always good when it ends in positive result.

14. Global attraction is a function of an outstanding character and distinction .

15. In the journey of discovery , never let compliments get to your head and never let criticism get to your heart .

16. True love is eternally addicted to truth and forever allergic to lies

17. The silence of God in your life ,is not the absence of God in your situation .

18. Whenever you make God a priority in your life , God makes you a superiority .

19. In the journey of destiny , every new level brings a new devil.

20 . Intimacy with God in your relationship with him ,reduces the effects of storms in your journey of life .

21. Every right man knows what he wants in a woman but every wrong man doesn't .

22. one of the real proves of love is investment of time and sacrifices

23 what you keep looking at is what you keep looking like . What do you see.?

23."marriage is the highest for of friendship on earth , marry your friend ."'

24. "Every future you are looking at to be now has an existing character lived already or on it now … so seek out such and model yours. .."

25 ".when your charisma exceeds your character, then, calamity is inevitable ."

26. "If you chase God the way you are chasing women , You will have a woman that chases God ."

27. "If you chase God the way you are chasing men , you will have a man that chases God ."

28. "Let your positive reactions cause a positive orientation in the life of those who come in contact with you . "

29. "When passion meets hunger , vision is born . "

30. "Many ladies are busy slaying to get a cute packaged man only few are deep in prayer to get the right man ."'

31. "emotion without a decision will end up in frustration."

32. "Never seek for a mega phone ,while still in incubating process , for conception takes 9 months before delivery "

33. "Consistency conceives commitment, commitment births focus and focus eliminates competition "

34. ''Many are busy chasing activities but only few are busy maximizing opportunities and impacting destinies ''

35.''To eat the seed for the future now is to live a life of hunger in the future tomorrow.''

36. ''To live in this surprised world surprised, is to surprise yourself with a surprise of disappointment ''coined from my role model Dr, Paul Enenche .

37. ''To place your confidence in a fellow man without placing such to divinity first , is a direct signature for frustration'' .

38. "Disconnection from the right company produces obscurity and invites calamity "

39. "Don't be over confident of your convictions, as long as you are not careful of association"

40. "In the quest of love , just be the right person and you will attract your right choice ..."

41. "Stop waiting for the perfect soul mate , just be the right person and you will attract your right choice "

42. " Never seek for a mega phone ,while still in incubating process, conceptions takes 9 months before delivery "

43. " The purpose of relationship is not to have another who might complete you, but to have another with whom you might share your completeness "

44. "when you reject one because of his or her weakness , you have invariably rejected his or her strength "

45. " the power of relationship is in love and the power of friendship is in communication and the power of communication is in sharing "

46. I have found the paradox that if I love until it hurts , then there is

no hurt but only more love" .... coined from mother Teresa.

47. " strength is not the ability to destroy the things you hate ;but true strength is the ability to build the things you love "

48 "A man's visible fat account may not be equal to his invisible mental (purpose) account".

49. "A week of neglect in life can lead to a month of regret and a year of frustration "
50."A man's life is a summation of his thoughts built in his mental capacity "
51. "Love alone cannot sustain and keep a relationship but deeper understanding and wisdom "
52. most times your heart needs more time to accept what your mind already knows and wants because the mind is always ahead of the brain "
53." Right mentality attracts prosperity just as sense secures supplies "
54." if your association doesn't accelerate your assignment , binding satan against retardation will be a sign for lack of wisdom "
55."persistence cures resistance   and grants access to inheritance "
56.You know an intelligent entity by what such says ,but you know a wise entity by the steps {actions } such takes "
57.Never engage into a relationship where you cant express your feelings , ideas and opinions "
58.To be in a relationship where you can't be yourself is to live like a prisoner of your imagination "

ABOUT THE BOOK

This book " **THE POWER OF POSITIVE MIND** " is well articulated, with great forwards and reviews from great minds and powerful informed and educated personalities and structured with some great insights and ideas strategically placed to shift Every youth

in this 21st century that is of noise and contradictions which is causing a great battles in their facets of life and to their place of assignments as a result of the daily battles that they fight ,loose ,win and give up in their minds to be ableto come to a place of boldness and take back their mind and also thosefacing what I call internal war with many issues of life due to lots offactors and government policies and corruptions in the social – economy system and such tends to live as a mediocre and exhibit average life ,the challenges such faces pushes him or her into deeper thinking and drawing a comparison from his mates in other continentsand as such becomes so defeated physically not knowing that the origin and beginning of the battle was first fought and lost in the field of the body system called THE MIND.

It will challenge your mental shifting capacity against the. System of the world today that tends to work against your locomotive dimension.

 As you study through may your inner eyes called your MIND be open and may you discover what your physical sights cannot see. .

ABOUT THE AUTHOR

Job Samuel chibuisi is a simple young Respected relationship and leadership motivational public speaker and the president of singles searching and waiting non governmental organisation currently in Nigeria and Europe and business Facebook page (Doc.Sam Relationship & Leadership Digest) with over 15,000 Social media followers ,He is a mentor and teacher (counsellor) to many Youths across the world ,

He has held and spoken in various seminars, conferences , religious gatherings, youth submits , groups and platforms in Africa , North America , South America, and Europe , He is a Nigerian ,Rivers state and 2nd Son to Late Mr & Mrs Florence O. Ihunwo in Port Harcourt CITY local Government Area , West Africa But Currently Resides In Constanta, Romania , Eastern Europe .

He is an author of five recent published selling books and also the innovator of the group called TUI ,the unique initiators currently operating in Europe with great minds. He, Holds Masters Degrees In Offshore Oil & Gas technology & management,Europe , B.sc in microbiology from Rivers state University of science and Technology , Nigeria , 2nd Bsc in navigation and water transport from Constanta Maritime University Romania (Europe), Diploma in Relationship and humanity (awarded by Constanta Maritime University on international scientific day 2017).

He also holds ministerial certificate in the Redeemed Christian Church of God (RCCG) , Certificate of General Administration in Nigerian Fellowship Of Evangelical Students (NIFES) 2014, diploma in leadership and entrepreneurship globally, certificate in public speaking and communication by Young Africans leaders initiative (YALI) USA and lots more awards and certificates in both public, religious and NGOs and Business sectors ,.Such as maritime certificates and professional courses and certificates as related to Maritime firms , oil and gas managements and administrations , and also some leadership and business certificates from Duke University ,

North Carolina. , USA , Recognition certificate from P2global leadership and entrepreneurs konsult United Kingdom.

FOR MORE DETAILS ; follow him up on
WWW.SSW.ORG/WIX.COM

IG ;
@Officialdoc_s
am

 Facebook; @

Job Samuel

Youtube:
@samuel c. Job

Facebook NGO and fan page: singles
searching and waiting ,SSW Facebook
Business facebook   page :
@DOCSAM246

yes
I want morebooks!

Buy your books fast and straightforward online - at one of world's fastest growing online book stores! Environmentally sound due to Print-on-Demand technologies.

Buy your books online at
www.morebooks.shop

Kaufen Sie Ihre Bücher schnell und unkompliziert online – auf einer der am schnellsten wachsenden Buchhandelsplattformen weltweit! Dank Print-On-Demand umwelt- und ressourcenschonend produziert.

Bücher schneller online kaufen
www.morebooks.shop

KS OmniScriptum Publishing
Brivibas gatve 197
LV-1039 Riga, Latvia
Telefax: +371 686 204 55

info@omniscriptum.com
www.omniscriptum.com

Printed by Books on Demand GmbH, Norderstedt / Germany